PISA

TOUR GUIDE 2024 AND BEYOND

Your Comprehensive Travel Companion to Exploring Culture, Hidden Gems, Cuisine and Local Secrets in the Heart of Tuscany – Packed with Detailed Maps & Itinerary Planner

BY

JAMES W. PATRICK

Copyright © 2024 by James W. Patrick. All rights reserved. The content of this work, including but not limited to text, images, and other media, is owned by James W. Patrick and is protected under copyright laws and international agreements. No part of this work may be reproduced, shared, or transmitted in any form or by any means without the explicit written consent of James W. Patrick. Unauthorized use, duplication, or distribution of this material may lead to legal action, including both civil and criminal penalties. For permission requests or further inquiries, please reach out to the author via the contact details provided in the book or on the author's official page.

TABLE OF CONTENTS

Copyright..1
My Experience in Pisa..5
Pisa FAQ..7
Why Visit Pisa?..10
What to Expect from this Guide...12

CHAPTER 1. INTRODUCTION TO PISA..16
1.1 Pisa: A Brief History...16
1.2 Geography and Climate...18
1.3 Getting to Know Pisa's Neighborhoods..20
1.4 Local Customs and Etiquette...22
1.5 Best Times to Visit...24

CHAPTER 2. ACCOMMODATION OPTIONS......................................26
2.1 Luxury Hotels and Resorts...26
2.2 Boutique and Design Hotels...28
2.3 Budget-Friendly Accommodations..30
2.4 Bed and Breakfasts..33
2.5 Unique Stays: Agriturismos and Vineyard Retreats............................35

CHAPTER 3. TRANSPORTATION IN PISA...37
3.1 Public Transport Networks...37
3.2 Taxis and Ride-Sharing Services...39
3.3 Renting a Car or Bike...41
3.4 Walking Tours and Guided Transportation...43
3.5 Accessibility Considerations for Travelers...45

CHAPTER 4. TOP ATTRACTIONS/HIDDEN GEMS.............................48
4.1 The Leaning Tower of Pisa...48
4.2 Piazza dei Miracoli (Square of Miracles)..50
4.3 Museums and Galleries..52
4.4 Parks and Gardens...54
4.5 Hidden Gems: Off-the-Beaten-Path Discoveries................................56

CHAPTER 5 PRACTICAL INFORMATION AND TRAVEL RESOURCES...........59
5.1 Maps and Navigation..59

5.2 Essential Packing List..61
5.3 Visa Requirements and Entry Procedures...63
5.4 Safety Tips and Emergency Contacts..65
5.5 Currency, Banking, Budgeting and Money Matters...67
5.6 Language, Communication and Useful Phrases... 69
5.7 Useful Websites, Mobile Apps and Online Resources....................................70
5.8 Visitor Centers and Tourist Assistance.. 72

CHAPTER 6. CULINARY DELIGHTS..75
6.1 Traditional Tuscan Cuisine...75
6.2 Local Delicacies and Street Food.. 77
6.3 Dining Experiences: Restaurants and Trattorias... 78
6.4 Wine Tasting and Vineyard Tours.. 80
6.4 Cooking Classes and Culinary Workshops..82

CHAPTER 7. CULTURE AND HERITAGE... 84
7.1 Historical Landmarks and Monuments.. 84
7.2 Art and Architecture... 86
7.3 Religious Sites and Traditions..87
7.4 Cultural Events and Festivals.. 89
7.5 Preservation Efforts and Heritage Conservation..91

CHAPTER 8. OUTDOOR ACTIVITIES AND ADVENTURES.....................................93
8.1 Walking Tours and Sightseeing..93
8.2 Cycling Routes and Bike Tours..95
8.3 River Cruises and Boat Tours..95
8.4 Hiking Trails and Nature Reserves.. 97
8.5 Adventure Sports: Climbing, Rafting, etc.. 98
8.6 Family and Kids Friendly Activities...100
8.7 Activities for Solo Travelers... 103

CHAPTER 9. SHOPPING IN PISA... 106
9.1 Local Markets and Street Vendors...106
9.2 Souvenir Shops and Artisanal Crafts... 108
9.3 Fashion Boutiques and Designer Stores..110
9.4 Specialty Food Stores and Delicatessens..112
9.5 Shopping Districts and Malls..114

CHAPTER 10. DAY TRIPS AND EXCURSIONS 116
10.1 Florence: The Cradle of the Renaissance 116
10.2 Lucca: Medieval Charm and City Walls 118
10.3 Cinque Terre: Coastal Beauty and Hiking Trails 119
10.4 Siena: Gothic Architecture and Palio Festival 121
10.5 Livorno: Port City and Maritime History 123

CHAPTER 11. ENTERTAINMENT AND NIGHTLIFE 125
11.1 Restaurants: Gastronomic Experiences 125
11.2 Bars and Pubs: Local Hangouts 127
11.3 Nightclubs and Live Music Venues 129
11.4 Cultural Performances and Shows 132
11.5 Safety Tips for Enjoying Pisa's Nightlife 134
Conclusion and Insider Tips for Visitors 136

PISA TRAVEL PLANNER 138

MY EXPERIENCE IN PISA

I've always sought to uncover the beating heart of each destination I visit, which led me to this one. From bustling metropolises to serene landscapes, I've traversed the globe in search of unique experiences that stir the soul and ignite the imagination. Yet, of all the places I've had the privilege to explore, none quite captured my fascination like the enchanting city of Pisa. Strategically located in the heart of Tuscany, Italy, Pisa is a treasure trove of history, culture, and architectural marvels. However, it was not merely the promise of iconic landmarks that drew me to this storied city; it was the allure of uncovering its hidden gems and immersing myself in its rich tapestry of tradition and heritage.

As I strolled through the cobblestone streets of Pisa, I was immediately struck by the palpable sense of history that permeated the air. Every corner seemed to whisper tales of bygone eras, beckoning me to delve deeper into its mysteries. Of course, no visit to Pisa would be complete without paying homage to its most famous resident: the Leaning Tower. Standing proudly in the Piazza dei Miracoli, this architectural marvel is a testament to human ingenuity and the enduring spirit of resilience. As I gazed upon its slanted silhouette against the backdrop of an azure sky, I couldn't help but marvel at the sheer audacity of its creators.

Yet, it was not merely the sight of the Leaning Tower that left me spellbound; it was the experience of climbing its spiraling staircase and feeling the weight of history beneath my feet. With each step, I was transported back in time, imagining the countless souls who had ascended these same stairs centuries before me. From the top of the tower, the panoramic view of Pisa spread out before me like a patchwork quilt, each building a testament to the city's enduring legacy. The Cathedral, with its pristine white façade and intricate marble carvings, stood as a symbol of faith and devotion, while the Baptistery, with its ornate architecture and exquisite acoustics, seemed to resonate with the echoes of centuries past.

Yet, as mesmerizing as the architectural wonders of Pisa were, it was the warmth and hospitality of its people that truly captured my heart. From the jovial street vendors hawking their wares to the passionate artisans honing their craft, every interaction felt like a glimpse into the soul of this vibrant city. One of the highlights of my journey was stumbling upon a quaint trattoria tucked away in a quiet alleyway. As I savored the flavors of freshly made pasta and locally sourced ingredients, I couldn't help but marvel at the simple joys of life that Pisa had to offer. It was a reminder that amidst the grandeur of its monuments, it was the authentic experiences and connections forged with its inhabitants that made Pisa truly special.

As I bid farewell to Pisa, I carried with me not only memories that would last a lifetime but also a newfound appreciation for the power of travel to enrich the mind, body, and soul. For anyone seeking a journey off the beaten path, I cannot recommend Pisa highly enough. Whether you're an avid history buff, a connoisseur of fine cuisine, or simply a seeker of beauty in all its forms, Pisa has something to offer for everyone.

So, to all those who yearn to embark on a voyage of discovery, I implore you to set your sights on Pisa. Let its ancient streets be your guide, its towering monuments your muse, and its welcoming embrace your home away from home. Trust me when I say, the journey will be nothing short of extraordinary.

PISA FAQ

1. What is Pisa famous for?

Pisa is most famous for its iconic Leaning Tower, a symbol of architectural ingenuity and historical significance. However, it is also renowned for its rich history, stunning cathedral, and vibrant cultural scene.

2. How do I get to Pisa?

Pisa is easily accessible by air, with the Galileo Galilei International Airport serving as the main gateway. Additionally, train services connect Pisa to major Italian cities such as Florence, Rome, and Venice, making it a convenient stop on any itinerary.

3. When is the best time to visit Pisa?

The best time to visit Pisa is during the spring and fall months (April to June and September to October), when the weather is pleasant and tourist crowds are smaller. However, Pisa can be enjoyed year-round, with each season offering its own unique charm.

4. How long should I spend in Pisa?

While it's possible to see the main attractions of Pisa in a day, I recommend spending at least two days to fully explore the city and its surrounding areas. This allows ample time to visit the Leaning Tower, explore the historic center, and savor the local cuisine.

5. Is the Leaning Tower safe to climb?

Yes, the Leaning Tower is safe to climb, but visitors should be aware that the staircase is narrow and can be quite steep. It's also important to note that only a limited number of visitors are allowed inside at a time, so it's advisable to book tickets in advance to avoid disappointment.

6. Can I take photos with the Leaning Tower?

Absolutely! In fact, no visit to Pisa is complete without the obligatory "holding up the Leaning Tower" photo. There are plenty of spots around the Piazza dei Miracoli where you can capture this iconic shot.

7. Are there any other attractions in Pisa besides the Leaning Tower?

Yes, Pisa boasts a wealth of attractions beyond the Leaning Tower. The Piazza dei Miracoli, where the tower is located, is also home to the stunning Pisa Cathedral and Baptistery. Additionally, the historic center of Pisa is dotted with charming churches, museums, and palaces waiting to be explored.

8. What should I eat in Pisa?

Pisa is known for its delicious Tuscan cuisine, characterized by fresh, locally sourced ingredients and simple yet flavorful dishes. Be sure to try specialties such as ribollita (a hearty vegetable soup), pappa al pomodoro (tomato and bread soup), and cecina (chickpea flatbread).

9. Is Pisa expensive to visit?

While Pisa can be a bit pricey compared to other Italian cities, it is still possible to enjoy a budget-friendly trip with careful planning. Look for affordable accommodations outside the city center, dine at local trattorias rather than touristy restaurants, and take advantage of free attractions such as walking tours and public parks.

10. Can I visit Pisa as a day trip from Florence?

Yes, Pisa makes for an excellent day trip from Florence, with frequent train services connecting the two cities in just about an hour. Spend the day exploring the highlights of Pisa before returning to Florence in the evening.

11. Are there any guided tours of Pisa available?

Yes, there are plenty of guided tours available in Pisa, ranging from walking tours of the historic center to wine tasting excursions in the surrounding countryside. Guided tours offer valuable insights into the city's history, culture, and cuisine, making for a memorable and informative experience.

12. Can I visit the Leaning Tower at night?
Although the Leaning Tower is not accessible to visitors at night, the Piazza dei Miracoli is beautifully illuminated after dark, offering a magical ambiance for evening strolls and photos.

13. Is Pisa wheelchair accessible?
Many of Pisa's main attractions, including the Leaning Tower and Piazza dei Miracoli, are wheelchair accessible. However, some historic buildings may have limited accessibility due to their age and architectural constraints. It's advisable to check with individual attractions beforehand to ensure a smooth visit.

14. What souvenirs should I buy in Pisa?
Popular souvenirs from Pisa include handcrafted leather goods, locally produced olive oil and wine, and traditional Tuscan ceramics. You can find these items at markets, boutiques, and artisan shops throughout the city.

15. What else can I do near Pisa?
In addition to exploring Pisa itself, there are plenty of day trip options available for those looking to venture beyond the city limits. Visit nearby towns such as Lucca, known for its intact Renaissance-era walls, or take a scenic drive through the picturesque Tuscan countryside.

Pisa, with its iconic Leaning Tower and rich cultural heritage, offers travelers a truly unforgettable experience. Whether you're marveling at architectural wonders, savoring delectable cuisine, or simply soaking in the vibrant atmosphere, Pisa has something to delight every traveler. So pack your bags, embark on an adventure, and discover the magic of Pisa for yourself!

WHY VISIT PISA?

Captivating History and Architecture

Imagine standing in the midst of a centuries-old square, surrounded by towering structures that whisper tales of times long past. This is the allure of Pisa, a city steeped in history and adorned with architectural wonders that defy the imagination. At the heart of Pisa lies the iconic Leaning Tower, an engineering marvel that has captured the world's fascination for generations. Its slanted silhouette against the azure sky serves as a poignant reminder of human ingenuity and the enduring spirit of resilience. But the Leaning Tower is just the beginning. Pisa's historic center is a labyrinth of narrow streets and hidden treasures, where every corner reveals a new chapter in the city's rich tapestry of tradition and heritage. From the majestic Pisa Cathedral to the elegant Baptistery, each monument is a testament to the city's illustrious past and a testament to the artisans who crafted them with unwavering dedication and skill.

Cultural Riches and Vibrant Atmosphere

Beyond its architectural splendors, Pisa is a city alive with culture and vibrancy, where the echoes of the past mingle harmoniously with the rhythms of modern life. Wander through the bustling markets and vibrant piazzas, where street performers serenade passersby and locals gather to socialize and savor the simple pleasures of life. Immerse yourself in the vibrant arts scene, where galleries and theaters showcase the talents of local artists and performers. Indulge your senses in the tantalizing aromas and flavors of Tuscan cuisine, from hearty pasta dishes to delicate pastries and gelato. In Pisa, every moment is an invitation to savor the richness of life and embrace the beauty of the world around you.

Warmth and Hospitality

But perhaps what truly sets Pisa apart is the warmth and hospitality of its people. Upon your arrival, you'll receive warm welcomes and sincere hospitality, entering into a community. that takes pride in sharing its culture and traditions with visitors from near and far. Strike up a conversation with a local artisan or join a group of friends for aperitivo in the evening, and you'll quickly discover that in Pisa, strangers are merely friends you haven't met yet. It's this sense of camaraderie and connection that makes Pisa feel like home, no matter where you come from or how far you've traveled.

Unforgettable Experiences

In Pisa, every step is a journey of discovery, every moment an opportunity for adventure. Climb to the top of the Leaning Tower and drink in the panoramic views of the city below. Stroll along the banks of the Arno River at sunset and watch as the golden light bathes the city in a warm glow. Lose yourself in the maze-like streets of the historic center, where hidden courtyards and ancient churches await around every corner. And when night falls, don't be afraid to wander off the beaten path and explore the city's hidden gems, from cozy wine bars to lively jazz clubs. In Pisa, the possibilities are endless, and the memories you'll create will last a lifetime.

In a world filled with wonders waiting to be explored, Pisa stands out as a destination like no other. With it's historic lively culture, and welcoming demeanor, it's a city that enchants the imagination and leaves an indelible mark on the heart. So why visit Pisa? Because here, amidst the beauty and splendor of centuries past, you'll find not just a destination, but an experience that will stay with you long after you've said goodbye. Come, discover the enchantment of Pisa for yourself, and let its magic ignite your spirit and awaken your sense of wonder.

WHAT TO EXPECT FROM THIS GUIDE

Enter the captivating city of Pisa, where history, art, and architectural marvels blend harmoniously. As an author of numerous travel guides, it is my pleasure to present to you the ultimate resource for exploring Pisa and its surrounding treasures in 2024 and beyond. In this comprehensive guide, you'll discover everything you need to know to make the most of your visit, from navigating the city's charming streets to indulging in its culinary delights and immersing yourself in its rich heritage.

Maps and Navigation
Navigating the streets of Pisa is a breeze, thanks to its compact size and well-marked attractions. Upon arrival, pick up a map from the tourist information center or download a digital map to your smartphone for easy reference. The city center is easily walkable, allowing you to explore its hidden corners and historic landmarks at your own pace. For longer journeys, Pisa offers a reliable public transportation system, including buses and trains, connecting you to nearby towns and attractions.

Accommodation Options
Pisa provides a variety of lodging choices to accommodate every budget and preference, from luxury hotels with breathtaking views of the Leaning Tower to cozy bed and breakfasts tucked away in historic buildings, there's something for everyone. For a truly authentic experience, consider staying in a traditional Tuscan villa or agriturismo in the countryside, where you can immerse yourself in the region's natural beauty and tranquility.

Transportation
Getting to and around Pisa is easy, thanks to its well-connected transportation network. The Galileo Galilei International Airport serves as the main gateway to the city, with direct flights from major European cities and beyond. Once in Pisa, you can easily explore the city on foot, by bike, or using public transportation. Renting a car is also a

convenient option for exploring the surrounding countryside and nearby attractions at your own pace.

Top Attractions

Of course, no visit to Pisa would be complete without marveling at its most famous landmark: the Leaning Tower. Perched on the stunning Piazza dei Miracoli, this architectural marvel is a must-see for any visitor. Be sure to also explore the nearby Pisa Cathedral and Baptistery, both of which are renowned for their exquisite architecture and historical significance. Other notable attractions include the picturesque River Arno, the charming Piazza dei Cavalieri, and the vibrant Borgo Stretto with its bustling cafes and shops.

Practical Information and Travel Resources

Before embarking on your journey to Pisa, it's important to be prepared with some practical information. The currency used in Italy is the Euro (€), and most establishments accept major credit cards. English is widely spoken in tourist areas, but it's always helpful to learn a few basic Italian phrases. Don't forget to check visa requirements for your country of origin and ensure you have adequate travel insurance coverage.

Culinary Delights

One of the highlights of any trip to Pisa is indulging in its delicious cuisine. From hearty Tuscan classics like ribollita and pappa al pomodoro to fresh seafood dishes and mouthwatering gelato, there's no shortage of culinary delights to tempt your taste buds. Be sure to sample local specialties like cecina (chickpea flatbread), lampredotto (tripe sandwich), and of course, the region's famous wines, such as Chianti and Brunello di Montalcino.

Culture and Heritage

Pisa is steeped in history and culture, with a rich heritage dating back centuries. Explore its fascinating museums, art galleries, and historic landmarks to uncover the city's storied past. Don't miss the opportunity to attend a classical music concert or opera performance in one of Pisa's magnificent theaters, or immerse yourself in local traditions and festivals celebrating everything from food and wine to art and music.

Outdoor Activities and Adventures

For outdoor enthusiasts, Pisa offers a wealth of activities to enjoy amidst its stunning natural surroundings. Take a leisurely bike ride along the banks of the River Arno, hike through the picturesque hills of the Tuscan countryside, or enjoy a scenic boat tour along the coast. Adventurous travelers can also try their hand at rock climbing, horseback riding, or even hot air ballooning for a bird's eye view of the breathtaking landscape.

Shopping

No visit to Pisa would be complete without a bit of shopping. Explore the city's charming boutiques, artisan workshops, and bustling markets to find unique souvenirs and gifts to take home. From handcrafted leather goods and ceramics to locally produced olive oil and wine, you're sure to find something special to remember your time in Pisa.

Day Trips and Excursions

While Pisa itself has plenty to offer, don't miss the opportunity to explore the surrounding area on a day trip or excursion. Visit nearby towns and villages such as Lucca, known for its intact Renaissance-era walls, or venture further afield to the breathtaking Cinque Terre coastline or the historic city of Florence, both easily accessible by train or car.

Entertainment and Nightlife

As the sun sets over Pisa, the city comes alive with a vibrant nightlife scene. Enjoy a leisurely dinner at a cozy trattoria or indulge in a cocktail at one of the city's chic bars and lounges. For those looking to dance the night away, Pisa offers a variety of clubs and discos where you can party into the wee hours of the morning.

Pisa is a city of endless wonders waiting to be discovered. Whether you're drawn to its iconic landmarks, its rich history and culture, or its mouthwatering cuisine and vibrant nightlife, there's something for everyone to enjoy. So pack your bags, embark on an adventure, and prepare to be captivated by the beauty and charm of Pisa and beyond. Your unforgettable Tuscan journey awaits!

CHAPTER 1

INTRODUCTION TO PISA

1.1 Pisa: A Brief History

Nestled in the heart of Tuscany, Italy, Pisa is a city steeped in history and tradition, its roots reaching back through the annals of time. From its humble beginnings as a modest Etruscan settlement to its rise as a maritime powerhouse and cultural epicenter, the story of Pisa is as captivating as the city itself.

Ancient Origins and Etruscan Legacy

The history of Pisa dates back over two millennia, with evidence of human habitation dating as far back as the Bronze Age. However, it was during the Etruscan period, around the 6th century BCE, that Pisa began to emerge as a significant settlement. Situated strategically along the banks of the Arno River, Pisa thrived as a trading hub and center of commerce, its fortunes intertwined with those of neighboring Etruscan cities.

Medieval Powerhouse and Maritime Supremacy

By the Middle Ages, Pisa had established itself as a formidable maritime power, its navy dominating the Mediterranean and beyond. The city's wealth and influence grew exponentially, fueled by trade with North Africa, the Middle East, and the Byzantine Empire. It was during this period of prosperity that many of Pisa's iconic landmarks, including the Leaning Tower, Cathedral, and Baptistery, were constructed, their grandeur serving as a testament to the city's burgeoning wealth and ambition.

Rivalries and Conflicts

However, Pisa's ascent to power was not without its challenges. Throughout the Middle Ages, the city found itself embroiled in bitter rivalries with neighboring city-states, most notably Genoa and Florence. These conflicts, fueled by territorial disputes and economic competition, would ultimately shape the course of Pisan history, leading to periods of conquest, defeat, and resurgence.

Decline and Renaissance Revival

By the 15th century, Pisa's golden age had come to an end, its fortunes waning in the face of internal strife, external pressures, and shifting trade routes. The city fell under the control of Florence in 1406, marking the beginning of a long period of decline. However, despite its diminished stature, Pisa continued to play a significant role in the cultural and intellectual life of Italy, its university attracting scholars and thinkers from across Europe during the Renaissance.

Modern Era and Cultural Renaissance

In the centuries that followed, Pisa experienced a cultural renaissance of sorts, its historic landmarks and architectural treasures drawing visitors and admirers from around the world. The 19th and 20th centuries saw efforts to preserve and restore Pisa's heritage, culminating in the city's designation as a UNESCO World Heritage Site in 1987. Today, Pisa stands as a living testament to its rich and storied past, its streets alive with the echoes of centuries gone by.

Visiting Pisa

For visitors to Pisa, the city's rich history is palpable at every turn. From the majestic Leaning Tower to the awe-inspiring Cathedral and Baptistery, Pisa's historic landmarks offer a glimpse into its illustrious past. Exploring the city's winding streets and picturesque squares, visitors can immerse themselves in its vibrant culture and heritage, discovering hidden gems and ancient treasures around every corner.

The history of Pisa is a tapestry woven from the threads of time, its story a testament to the resilience, creativity, and spirit of its people. From its humble beginnings as an Etruscan settlement to its rise as a maritime powerhouse and cultural epicenter, Pisa's journey through the ages is a testament to the enduring allure of this captivating city. So come, wander its historic streets, marvel at its architectural wonders, and discover the magic of Pisa for yourself.

1.2 Geography and Climate

Geography of Pisa

Pisa boasts a captivating blend of natural beauty and historical charm. Situated along the tranquil banks of the River Arno, the city is renowned for its iconic landmarks, including the Leaning Tower, which stands as a testament to human ingenuity and the forces of nature. The city's layout reflects its ancient origins, with narrow cobblestone streets winding through the historic center, lined with centuries-old buildings adorned with ornate facades and wrought iron balconies.

Pisa's geographic location has long been strategic, serving as a hub of trade and commerce since ancient times. Its proximity to the Mediterranean Sea facilitated maritime trade routes, while its fertile lands supported agriculture and viticulture. Today, Pisa continues to thrive as a cultural and economic center, attracting visitors from around the globe eager to explore its rich history and vibrant atmosphere.

Beyond the city limits, the rolling hills and verdant valleys of the Tuscan countryside beckon travelers to explore its idyllic landscapes. Vineyards stretch as far as the eye can see, producing some of Italy's finest wines, while olive groves dot the horizon, yielding the prized olive oil that is integral to Tuscan cuisine. Charming hilltop villages and historic towns dot the landscape, offering a glimpse into rural life in Tuscany and providing endless opportunities for exploration and discovery.

Climate of Pisa

Pisa enjoys a Mediterranean climate characterized by mild winters and warm, sunny summers, making it an ideal destination for visitors year-round. Spring arrives in Pisa with a burst of color, as flowers bloom and trees come to life after the winter months. Temperatures begin to rise, with daytime highs averaging in the comfortable 60s to 70s Fahrenheit (15-25 degrees Celsius). This is an ideal time to explore Pisa's outdoor attractions, from the historic Piazza dei Miracoli to the scenic banks of the River Arno.

Summer

Summer brings sunshine and warmth to Pisa, with long, sunny days perfect for sightseeing and outdoor activities. Temperatures often climb into the 80s and 90s Fahrenheit (high 20s to low 30s Celsius), prompting locals and visitors alike to seek refuge from the heat in shaded piazzas or along the cool waterfront. Despite the heat, summer is a vibrant time in Pisa, with festivals, concerts, and cultural events filling the city's streets and squares.

Fall

Fall is a magical time in Pisa, as the summer crowds begin to thin and the city is bathed in the golden light of autumn. Temperatures gradually cool, with crisp mornings giving way to mild afternoons perfect for exploring the city's historic treasures. Fall is also harvest season in Tuscany, with vineyards and olive groves buzzing with activity as locals gather grapes and olives for the year's harvest.

Winter

Winter in Pisa is mild compared to many other parts of Europe, with temperatures rarely dropping below freezing. While the occasional rain shower is not uncommon, winter days are often bright and sunny, providing ample opportunities for exploring Pisa's indoor attractions, such as museums, galleries, and churches. The holiday season brings festive cheer to the city, with Christmas markets, concerts, and seasonal decorations adorning the streets and squares.

The geography and climate of Pisa combine to create a destination that is as diverse as it is enchanting. Whether you're drawn to its historic landmarks, its scenic landscapes, or its vibrant culture, Pisa offers something for every traveler to discover and enjoy.

1.3 Getting to Know Pisa's Neighborhoods

As you embark on your journey to Pisa, prepare to be enchanted by the the city's varied and lively neighborhoods, each with its own distinct atmosphere and attractions from the historic center with its iconic landmarks to the charming outskirts dotted with vineyards and olive groves, Pisa's neighborhoods invite exploration and discovery, promising unforgettable experiences at every turn.

Historic Center

At the heart of Pisa lies its historic center, a maze of narrow cobblestone streets, ancient churches, and medieval squares. Here, you'll find the iconic Piazza dei Miracoli (Square of Miracles), home to the Leaning Tower, Pisa Cathedral, Baptistery, and Camposanto Monumentale. Lose yourself in the winding alleys of Borgo Stretto, lined with shops, cafes, and artisan boutiques, or marvel at the grandeur of Piazza dei Cavalieri, once the political center of medieval Pisa. The historic center is also home to vibrant markets, bustling piazzas, and hidden gems waiting to be discovered around every corner.

San Francesco

Located just south of the historic center, the San Francesco neighborhood offers a quieter and more residential atmosphere. Here, you'll find tranquil parks, leafy boulevards, and charming residential streets lined with elegant mansions and historic palaces. Don't miss the opportunity to explore the Giardino Scotto, a lush green oasis in the heart of the city, or visit the Church of San Francesco, known for its stunning frescoes and peaceful cloister.

Santa Maria

To the north of the historic center lies the Santa Maria neighborhood, a busy area celebrated for its lively markets, iconic squares, and vibrant street atmosphere. Explore the colorful stalls of the Mercato delle Vettovaglie, where locals gather to shop for fresh produce, meats, and cheeses, or wander through the historic Piazza delle Vettovaglie, home to some of Pisa's oldest buildings and charming cafes. For a taste of local cuisine, head to Via San Martino, where trattorias and osterias serve up traditional Tuscan dishes and regional specialties.

Monti Pisani

Venture beyond the city center to the Monti Pisani, a picturesque region of rolling hills, vineyards, and olive groves just south of Pisa. Here, you'll find charming hilltop villages such as Calci and Vicopisano, each offering stunning views of the surrounding countryside and a glimpse into rural Tuscan life. Explore ancient churches, historic castles, and scenic hiking trails that wind through forests and along riverbanks, providing endless opportunities for outdoor adventure and exploration.

Marina di Pisa

For those seeking sun, sand, and sea, Marina di Pisa offers the perfect escape. Located just a short drive from the city center, this seaside resort town boasts immaculate beaches, glistening turquoise waters, and a bustling waterfront lined with restaurants, cafes, and shops.Spend your days soaking up the sun on the sandy shores, swimming in the refreshing waters of the Tyrrhenian Sea, or indulging in fresh seafood and gelato at one of the waterfront eateries.

As you can see, Pisa's neighborhoods are as diverse as they are captivating, each offering its own unique blend of history, culture, and charm. Whether you're exploring the historic center with its iconic landmarks, wandering through the leafy streets of San Francesco, or soaking up the sun in Marina di Pisa, you're sure to be captivated by the beauty and allure of this enchanting city. So pack your bags, lace up your walking shoes, and prepare to embark on a journey of discovery through the vibrant neighborhoods of Pisa. Your adventure awaits!

1.4 Local Customs and Etiquette

As you prepare to immerse yourself in the rich culture and heritage of Pisa, it's important to familiarize yourself with the local customs and etiquette. By respecting the traditions of the city and its inhabitants, you'll not only deepen your understanding of Pisan culture but also forge meaningful connections with the people you encounter along your journey.

Greeting and Interaction

In Pisa, greeting others with warmth and respect is highly valued. When meeting someone for the first time, a firm handshake and direct eye contact are customary, accompanied by a friendly "Buongiorno" (good morning) or "Buonasera" (good evening), depending on the time of day. It's also common to exchange kisses on the cheek as a sign of affection, though this may vary depending on the relationship and context. During conversations, Pisans appreciate politeness and courtesy, so be sure to listen attentively, avoid interrupting, and express gratitude for any hospitality extended to you. Remember to address people by their title and surname unless invited to use their first name, and always wait for others to initiate more familiar forms of address.

Dining Etiquette

Sharing a meal with friends and family is a cherished tradition in Pisa, and dining etiquette reflects this sense of hospitality and conviviality. When invited to someone's home for a meal, it's customary to arrive on time or slightly early and to bring a small gift, such as a bottle of wine or dessert, as a token of appreciation. At the table, Pisans value good manners and moderation, so be sure to wait until everyone is seated before beginning to eat, and refrain from talking with your mouth full or reaching across the table for food. When offered a dish, it's polite to take a small portion and to express your enjoyment of the meal with compliments to the host or chef.

Respecting Cultural Sites

Pisa is home to a wealth of historic and cultural landmarks, from the iconic Leaning Tower to the majestic Pisa Cathedral. When visiting these sites, it's essential to show respect for their significance and sanctity. Dress modestly and appropriately, covering shoulders and knees, and refrain from loud or disruptive behavior that may disturb others or detract from the solemnity of the surroundings. Additionally, be mindful of any rules or regulations governing the use of photography or electronic devices, as some sites may have restrictions to preserve their integrity and protect sensitive artifacts. Remember to tread lightly and leave no trace, ensuring that future generations can continue to appreciate these treasures for years to come.

Navigating Social Situations

In social situations, Pisans value authenticity and sincerity, so it's important to be genuine and respectful in your interactions. If invited to a social gathering or event, be sure to RSVP promptly and arrive punctually, as tardiness is considered impolite. While alcohol may be served at social occasions, moderation is key, and excessive drinking is generally frowned upon. When saying goodbye, it's customary to offer a warm farewell and express your gratitude for the hospitality extended to you. A simple "Grazie mille" (thank you very much) accompanied by a handshake or kiss on the cheek is appropriate, depending on the level of familiarity with the individual.

By familiarizing yourself with the local customs and etiquette of Pisa, you'll not only show respect for the traditions of the city and its inhabitants but also enhance your overall experience as a visitor. By embracing the values of warmth, respect, and conviviality, you'll forge meaningful connections with the people you meet and gain a deeper understanding of the rich culture and heritage that make Pisa truly unique. So as you embark on your journey through the streets of Pisa, remember to tread lightly, speak kindly, and embrace the customs that make this city a welcoming and vibrant destination for travelers from around the world.

1.5 Best Time to Visit

Embarking on a journey to Pisa is an adventure filled with culture, history, and architectural wonders. However, to make the most of your experience, it's essential to consider the timing of your visit. From the vibrant festivals of summer to the tranquility of winter, each season offers its own unique charm and opportunities for exploration in Pisa.

Spring

As the winter chill gives way to warmer temperatures, spring emerges as one of the best times to visit Pisa. From March to May, the city comes alive with the vibrant colors of blooming flowers and lush greenery. With mild temperatures ranging from the 50s to 70s Fahrenheit (10-20 degrees Celsius), spring is perfect for leisurely strolls through Pisa's historic streets and iconic landmarks, such as the Leaning Tower and Piazza dei Miracoli. Additionally, spring marks the beginning of festival season in Pisa, with events celebrating everything from art and music to food and wine.

Summer

Summer in Pisa is synonymous with sunshine, outdoor activities, and lively festivities. From June to August, the city basks in warm temperatures, with highs reaching into the 80s and 90s Fahrenheit (high 20s to low 30s Celsius). While the summer months can be hot and crowded, they also offer the perfect opportunity to soak up the sun on the beaches of Marina di Pisa or enjoy al fresco dining in the city's charming piazzas. Be sure to check out the various summer festivals and events, including the Luminara di San Ranieri, a spectacular procession of illuminated boats on the River Arno, and the Pisa Music Festival, featuring performances by local and international artists.

Fall

As summer fades into fall, Pisa takes on a more tranquil and romantic atmosphere. From September to November, temperatures begin to cool, and the crowds thin out, making it an ideal time to explore the city's historic landmarks and cultural treasures without the hustle and bustle of peak tourist season. Fall also marks the grape and olive harvest in Tuscany, providing a unique opportunity to participate in traditional harvest activities and sample the region's renowned wines and olive oils.

Winter

Winter in Pisa is a time of quiet charm and festive cheer. From December to February, temperatures dip into the 40s and 50s Fahrenheit (5-15 degrees Celsius), creating a cozy atmosphere perfect for exploring the city's museums, galleries, and historic sites. While some attractions may have reduced hours or be closed for renovations, winter offers the chance to experience Pisa's cultural treasures without the crowds. Be sure to visit during the holiday season to enjoy the festive decorations, Christmas markets, and seasonal events that bring the city to life with warmth and joy.

The best time to visit Pisa ultimately depends on your preferences and interests. Whether you're seeking the vibrant energy of summer festivals, the tranquility of a springtime stroll through historic streets, or the cozy charm of winter in Tuscany, Pisa offers something for every traveler to enjoy.

CHAPTER 2

ACCOMMODATION OPTIONS

Click the link or Scan QR Code with a device to view a comprehensive map of various Accommodation Options in Pisa – https://shorturl.at/rlX69

2.1 Luxury Hotels and Resorts

As you embark on your journey to the enchanting city of Pisa, why not elevate your experience with a stay at one of its luxurious hotels and resorts? Nestled amidst the historic charm and natural beauty of Tuscany, these exclusive accommodations offer unparalleled comfort, impeccable service, and unforgettable experiences, ensuring that your visit to Pisa is nothing short of extraordinary.

Grand Hotel Duomo

Located in the heart of Pisa's historic center, just steps away from the iconic Leaning Tower, the Grand Hotel Duomo offers a truly luxurious retreat. With elegantly appointed rooms and suites boasting stunning views of the city skyline, this five-star hotel exudes sophistication and style. Guests can indulge in gourmet cuisine at the hotel's rooftop restaurant, relax by the rooftop pool, or unwind with a massage at the spa. Prices for lodging at the Grand Hotel Duomo typically range from $200 to $500 per night, depending on the season and room category.

Relais Dell'Orologio

Situated in a historic building overlooking the Piazza dei Cavalieri, the Relais Dell'Orologio combines old-world charm with modern luxury. Each of the hotel's suites is elegantly furnished and features a unique blend of classic Tuscan décor and contemporary amenities. Guests can enjoy a sumptuous breakfast buffet in the hotel's courtyard garden, relax in the cozy library lounge, or sip cocktails at the rooftop bar while taking in panoramic views of the city. Prices for lodging at the Relais Dell'Orologio start at around $250 per night.

Bagni di Pisa

For those seeking a truly indulgent experience, the Bagni di Pisa offers the ultimate in luxury and relaxation. Located in the scenic countryside just outside of Pisa, this five-star resort features lavish spa facilities, including thermal pools, saunas, and wellness treatments inspired by ancient Roman traditions. Guests can unwind in opulent rooms and suites decorated with antique furnishings and marble bathrooms, dine on gourmet cuisine at the hotel's Michelin-starred restaurant, or explore the surrounding olive groves and vineyards. Prices for lodging at the Bagni di Pisa start at around $300 per night.

NH Pisa

Conveniently located near Pisa's main train station and airport, the NH Pisa offers contemporary luxury with a focus on comfort and convenience. The hotel's sleek and stylish rooms are equipped with modern amenities, including flat-screen TVs, minibars, and free Wi-Fi. Guests can enjoy a delicious buffet breakfast each morning, work out at the fitness center, or relax with a drink at the hotel's bar. Prices for lodging at the NH Pisa typically range from $100 to $250 per night, making it a more affordable option for luxury travelers.

San Ranieri Hotel

Designed by world-renowned architect Gino Valle, the San Ranieri Hotel is a striking modern masterpiece located just outside of Pisa's city center. The hotel's sleek and minimalist design is complemented by luxurious amenities, including spacious rooms with floor-to-ceiling windows, a rooftop terrace with panoramic views, and a gourmet restaurant serving innovative Tuscan cuisine. Prices for lodging at the San Ranieri Hotel start at around $150 per night, making it a great option for travelers seeking style and sophistication at a reasonable price.

Hotel Relais Dell'Orologio

Nestled in the heart of Pisa's historic center, the Hotel Relais Dell'Orologio offers boutique luxury with a personalized touch. Housed in a beautifully restored 14th-century palace, the hotel features elegant rooms and suites decorated with antique furnishings and modern amenities. Guests can enjoy a complimentary breakfast each morning, relax in the hotel's charming courtyard garden, or take advantage of the concierge service to book tickets and reservations for local attractions. Prices for lodging at the Hotel Relais Dell'Orologio start at around $200 per night.

Whether you're looking for a luxurious getaway in the city center or a peaceful retreat in the Tuscan countryside, these luxurious hotels and resorts in Pisa offer the perfect blend of comfort, style, and indulgence. From rooftop pools and gourmet dining to lavish spas and personalized service, each property promises an unforgettable experience that will leave you feeling pampered and rejuvenated. So why wait? Treat yourself to the luxury you deserve and make your stay in Pisa truly exceptional.

2.2 Boutique and Design Hotels

As you embark on your journey to the enchanting city of Pisa, why not elevate your experience with a stay at one of its luxurious hotels and resorts? Nestled amidst the historic charm and natural beauty of Tuscany, these exclusive accommodations offer unparalleled comfort, impeccable service, and unforgettable experiences, ensuring that your visit to Pisa is nothing short of extraordinary.

Relais Dell'Orologio

Situated in a historic building overlooking the Piazza dei Cavalieri, the Relais Dell'Orologio combines old-world charm with modern luxury. Each of the hotel's suites is elegantly furnished and features a unique blend of classic Tuscan décor and contemporary amenities. Guests can enjoy a sumptuous breakfast buffet in the hotel's courtyard garden, relax in the cozy library lounge, or sip cocktails at the rooftop bar while taking in panoramic views of the city. Prices for lodging at the Relais Dell'Orologio start at around $250 per night.

Bagni di Pisa

For those seeking a truly indulgent experience, the Bagni di Pisa offers the ultimate in luxury and relaxation. Located in the scenic countryside just outside of Pisa, this five-star resort features lavish spa facilities, including thermal pools, saunas, and wellness treatments inspired by ancient Roman traditions. Guests can unwind in opulent rooms and suites decorated with antique furnishings and marble bathrooms, dine on gourmet cuisine at the hotel's Michelin-starred restaurant, or explore the surrounding olive groves and vineyards. Prices for lodging at the Bagni di Pisa start at around $300 per night.

NH Pisa

Conveniently located near Pisa's main train station and airport, the NH Pisa offers contemporary luxury with a focus on comfort and convenience. The hotel's sleek and stylish rooms are equipped with modern amenities, including flat-screen TVs, minibars, and free Wi-Fi. Guests can enjoy a delicious buffet breakfast each morning, work out at the fitness center, or relax with a drink at the hotel's bar. Prices for lodging at the NH Pisa typically range from $100 to $250 per night, making it a more affordable option for luxury travelers.

San Ranieri Hotel

Designed by world-renowned architect Gino Valle, the San Ranieri Hotel is a striking modern masterpiece located just outside of Pisa's city center. The hotel's sleek and minimalist design is complemented by luxurious amenities, including spacious rooms with floor-to-ceiling windows, a rooftop terrace with panoramic views, and a gourmet restaurant serving innovative Tuscan cuisine. Prices for lodging at the San Ranieri Hotel start at around $150 per night, making it a great option for travelers seeking style and sophistication at a reasonable price.

Hotel Relais Dell'Orologio

Nestled in the heart of Pisa's historic center, the Hotel Relais Dell'Orologio offers boutique luxury with a personalized touch. Housed in a beautifully restored 14th-century palace, the hotel features elegant rooms and suites decorated with antique furnishings and modern amenities. Guests can enjoy a complimentary breakfast each morning, relax in the hotel's charming courtyard garden, or take advantage of the concierge service to book tickets and reservations for local attractions. Prices for lodging at the Hotel Relais Dell'Orologio start at around $200 per night.

Whether you're seeking a lavish retreat in the heart of the city or a tranquil escape in the Tuscan countryside, these luxurious hotels and resorts in Pisa offer the perfect blend of comfort, style, and indulgence. From rooftop pools and gourmet dining to lavish spas and personalized service, each property promises an unforgettable experience that will leave you feeling pampered and rejuvenated. So why wait? Treat yourself to the luxury you deserve and make your stay in Pisa truly exceptional.

2.3 Budget-Friendly Accommodations

As a seasoned traveler, I understand the importance of finding comfortable yet affordable accommodations that don't break the bank. In Pisa, a city known for its rich history and architectural wonders, there are several budget-friendly options that offer great value for money without compromising on comfort or convenience. Whether you're a solo adventurer, a budget-conscious traveler, or a family seeking affordable lodging, Pisa has something to offer for every budget. When it comes to exploring a new destination like Pisa, finding the right place to stay can greatly enhance your travel experience. From charming guesthouses to budget-friendly hotels, the key is to seek accommodations that provide comfort, convenience, and affordability. In this guide, we'll explore five budget-friendly options in Pisa that offer cozy lodging, essential amenities, and a welcoming atmosphere for travelers on a budget.

1. Hotel Francesco

Located just a stone's throw away from the iconic Leaning Tower of Pisa, Hotel Francesco offers budget-friendly accommodations in the heart of the city. With its convenient location and affordable rates, this family-run hotel is ideal for travelers looking to explore Pisa's top attractions without breaking the bank. Prices for lodging start at around $50 per night for a standard double room, making it a budget-friendly option for solo travelers and couples alike. Amenities at Hotel Francesco include complimentary Wi-Fi, air conditioning, and a continental breakfast served daily. The hotel's unique feature lies in its friendly and attentive staff, who go above and beyond to ensure a pleasant stay for guests. Additionally, guests can take advantage of the hotel's tour desk to book excursions and explore Pisa's hidden gems with ease.

2. Hostel Pisa

For budget-conscious travelers seeking a sociable and lively atmosphere, Hostel Pisa is an excellent choice. Located within walking distance of Pisa Centrale train station, this hostel offers dormitory-style accommodations at affordable prices. Prices for lodging start at around $20 per night for a bed in a shared dormitory, making it one of the most budget-friendly options in the city. Amenities at Hostel Pisa include free Wi-Fi, a communal kitchen, and a cozy lounge area where guests can relax and mingle with fellow travelers. The hostel's unique feature is its vibrant social scene, with regular events and activities organized by the friendly staff. From pasta nights to city tours, there's always something exciting happening at Hostel Pisa.

3. Hotel La Pace

Nestled in a quiet residential area just a short walk from Pisa's historic center, Hotel La Pace offers affordable accommodations with a touch of elegance. Prices for lodging start at around $60 per night for a standard double room, making it an excellent choice for travelers seeking comfort and convenience on a budget. Amenities at Hotel La Pace include free Wi-Fi, air conditioning, and a continental breakfast served daily. The hotel's unique feature is its tranquil garden terrace, where guests can unwind after a day of sightseeing and enjoy a glass of wine amidst lush greenery. Additionally, the hotel offers bicycle rental services, allowing guests to explore Pisa's charming streets at their own pace.

4. B&B Hotel Pisa

Conveniently located near Pisa Centrale train station and within walking distance of the city center, B&B Hotel Pisa offers affordable accommodations with modern amenities. Prices for lodging start at around $50 per night for a standard double room, making it a budget-friendly option for both leisure and business travelers. Amenities at B&B Hotel Pisa include free Wi-Fi, air conditioning, and a buffet breakfast served daily. The hotel's unique feature is its pet-friendly policy, allowing guests to bring their furry friends along for the adventure. Additionally, the hotel offers secure parking facilities for guests arriving by car, providing added convenience and peace of mind.

5. Residence Antiche Navi Pisane

For travelers seeking a home away from home experience, Residence Antiche Navi Pisane offers cozy apartment-style accommodations at affordable prices. Located in a historic building near the Arno River, this residence is within walking distance of Pisa's main attractions. Prices for lodging start at around $70 per night for a studio apartment, making it a budget-friendly option for families and groups. Amenities at Residence Antiche Navi Pisane include fully-equipped kitchens, free Wi-Fi, and laundry facilities. The residence's unique feature is its charming courtyard garden, where guests can relax and soak up the Mediterranean sunshine. Additionally, the residence offers bicycle rental services, allowing guests to explore Pisa's picturesque streets and scenic waterfront paths.

Pisa offers a variety of budget-friendly accommodations that cater to the needs of every traveler. Whether you're looking for a centrally located hotel, a lively hostel, or a cozy apartment, there's something for everyone in this charming city. By choosing one of these budget-friendly options, you can enjoy a comfortable and affordable stay in Pisa without sacrificing quality or convenience. So pack your bags, book your stay, and get ready to explore all that Pisa has to offer on a budget-friendly budget.

2.4 Bed and Breakfasts

For travelers seeking a more intimate and personalized experience during their stay in Pisa, bed and breakfasts offer a warm and welcoming alternative to traditional hotels. Nestled in historic buildings and charming neighborhoods, these comfortable lodgings offer a welcoming atmosphere, allowing guests to fully embrace the local culture and hospitality of Pisa. Let's explore delightful bed and breakfasts that promise a memorable stay in this enchanting city.

1. Le Volte Antiche

Located in the heart of Pisa's historic center, Le Volte Antiche offers guests a cozy retreat in a beautifully restored 18th-century building. Each of the bed and breakfast's rooms is elegantly furnished and features traditional Tuscan décor, creating a warm and inviting atmosphere. Guests can enjoy a delicious homemade breakfast served in the charming dining room or relax in the peaceful courtyard garden. Prices for lodging at Le Volte Antiche start at around $80 per night, making it an affordable option for travelers seeking comfort and convenience in the heart of Pisa.

2. Villa Tower Inn

Situated just a short walk from the Leaning Tower of Pisa, Villa Tower Inn offers guests a tranquil escape in a historic villa surrounded by lush gardens. The bed and breakfast's spacious rooms are tastefully decorated and feature modern amenities, including air conditioning, flat-screen TVs, and free Wi-Fi. Guests can start their day with a complimentary breakfast buffet served in the elegant dining room or relax in the hotel's outdoor terrace overlooking the garden. Prices for lodging at Villa Tower Inn start at around $100 per night, making it a great choice for travelers seeking a peaceful retreat near Pisa's top attractions.

3. Il Toscano B&B

Located in the charming neighborhood of San Francesco, Il Toscano B&B offers guests a cozy and comfortable stay in a historic building dating back to the 16th century. The bed and breakfast's rooms are elegantly furnished and feature traditional Tuscan décor, creating a warm and inviting atmosphere. Guests can enjoy a delicious breakfast served in the hotel's dining room or relax in the communal lounge area with a book or a cup of coffee. Prices for lodging at Il Toscano B&B start at around $70 per night, making it an affordable option for travelers seeking a charming stay in Pisa's historic center.

4. B&B Guerrazzi

Situated just a short walk from Pisa's main train station, B&B Guerrazzi offers guests a convenient and comfortable stay in a historic building dating back to the 19th century. The bed and breakfast's rooms are tastefully decorated and feature modern amenities, including air conditioning, flat-screen TVs, and free Wi-Fi. Guests can enjoy a continental breakfast served in the hotel's cozy dining room or explore the nearby cafes and restaurants. Prices for lodging at B&B Guerrazzi start at around $60 per night, making it an excellent choice for budget-conscious travelers seeking convenience and comfort in Pisa.

5. La Papaya B&B

Located just a short drive from Pisa's city center, La Papaya B&B offers guests a peaceful retreat in a scenic countryside setting. The bed and breakfast's cozy rooms are decorated in a rustic style and feature private balconies overlooking the garden. Guests can enjoy a continental breakfast served in the hotel's dining room or relax in the outdoor pool surrounded by olive groves and vineyards. Prices for lodging at La Papaya B&B start at around $90 per night, making it an ideal choice for travelers seeking a tranquil escape from the hustle and bustle of the city.

With their warm hospitality, charming décor, and personalized service, bed and breakfasts offer travelers a unique and memorable experience during their stay in Pisa. From historic buildings in the heart of the city to peaceful retreats in the countryside, these delightful accommodations promise a cozy and comfortable stay that will leave guests feeling refreshed and rejuvenated. So why wait? Book your stay at one of these charming bed and breakfasts and discover the true essence of hospitality in Pisa.

2.5 Unique Stays: Agriturismos and Vineyard Retreats

Nestled amidst the stunning landscapes of Tasmania, agriturismos and vineyard retreats offer visitors a unique opportunity to experience the beauty of the countryside while immersing themselves in the region's rich agricultural heritage. From charming farm stays to luxurious vineyard estates, these unique accommodations provide a peaceful retreat from the hustle and bustle of city life, allowing guests to reconnect with nature and savor the flavors of Tasmania's bountiful land.

1. The Truffle Lodge

Located in the heart of the Derwent Valley, The Truffle Lodge offers guests a luxurious retreat amidst the pristine wilderness of Tasmania's southwest. Situated on a private 100-acre property, this eco-friendly lodge features spacious safari-style tents equipped with plush bedding, ensuite bathrooms, and private decks overlooking the Huon River. Guests can enjoy gourmet meals prepared using locally sourced ingredients, participate in truffle hunts and farm tours, or simply relax by the outdoor fireplace and stargaze under the clear night sky. Prices for lodging at The Truffle Lodge start at around $350 per night, including breakfast and select activities.

2. Freycinet Vineyard Retreat

Perched atop a hill overlooking the stunning Freycinet Peninsula, Freycinet Vineyard Retreat offers guests a luxurious escape in the heart of Tasmania's acclaimed wine region. Surrounded by acres of vineyards and olive groves, this boutique getaway offers sophisticated suites and cottages with sweeping views of the Hazards mountain range and Great Oyster Bay. Guests can indulge in wine tastings and vineyard tours, dine on gourmet cuisine at the on-site restaurant, or unwind with a massage at the spa. Prices for lodging at Freycinet Vineyard Retreat start at around $400 per night, including breakfast and select amenities.

3. Eagle's Nest Retreat

Hidden away in the picturesque Huon Valley, Eagle's Nest Retreat offers guests a secluded oasis surrounded by lush forests and rolling hills. The property features a collection of cozy cottages and eco-friendly cabins, each with its own private deck and outdoor hot tub overlooking the Huon River. Guests can explore the surrounding wilderness on guided bushwalks, kayak along the tranquil waters of the river, or simply relax and rejuvenate in the serene natural surroundings. Prices for lodging at Eagle's Nest Retreat start at around $250 per night, including breakfast and select activities.

4. Bruny Island Premium Wines
Situated on the idyllic Bruny Island, Bruny Island Premium Wines offers guests a unique opportunity to stay on a working vineyard and winery overlooking the D'Entrecasteaux Channel. The property features charming cottages with modern amenities and sweeping views of the surrounding countryside. Guests can sample award-winning wines at the cellar door, enjoy gourmet picnics in the vineyard, or explore the island's pristine beaches and rugged coastline. Prices for lodging at Bruny Island Premium Wines start at around $200 per night, including breakfast and select experiences.

5. Wilmot Hills Vineyard Retreat
Perched atop the rolling hills of northern Tasmania, Wilmot Hills Vineyard Retreat offers guests a peaceful escape in a picturesque rural setting. The property features boutique accommodation in a historic homestead and self-contained cottages, each with its own private verandah and stunning views of the vineyard and surrounding countryside. Guests can enjoy wine tastings and vineyard tours, relax by the fireplace with a glass of local wine, or explore the nearby national parks and hiking trails. Prices for lodging at Wilmot Hills Vineyard Retreat start at around $300 per night, including breakfast and select activities.

With their tranquil surroundings, luxurious accommodations, and immersive experiences, agriturismos and vineyard retreats in Tasmania offer guests a truly unique and unforgettable stay. Whether you're looking for a charming getaway, a wine-tasting experience, or simply a peaceful escape in nature, these distinctive properties provide the perfect setting to relax, unwind, and reconnect with the beauty of the Tasmanian countryside.

CHAPTER 3
TRANSPORTATION IN PISA

3.1 Public Transport Networks

As you embark on your journey to Pisa, navigating the city's public transport networks is essential for exploring its many attractions and landmarks. From buses to trains, Pisa offers a variety of convenient and affordable options for getting around the city and beyond. Let's delve into the details of Pisa's public transport networks to help you make the most of your visit.

Pisa People Mover

One of the most convenient modes of transportation in Pisa is the People Mover, a modern automated shuttle that connects Pisa Centrale railway station with the city's main attractions, including the Leaning Tower and Piazza dei Miracoli. Operating every few minutes, the People Mover provides a quick and efficient way to travel between the train station and the city center. Tickets for the People Mover cost around €1.50 for a one-way journey, making it an affordable option for visitors.

Local Buses

Pisa's local bus network offers comprehensive coverage of the city and its surrounding areas, providing an easy way to reach destinations not served by the People Mover. Managed by the Compagnia Pisana Trasporti (CPT), the bus network operates a variety of routes that connect neighborhoods, suburbs, and nearby towns. Visitors can purchase tickets directly from the bus driver or at designated ticket kiosks located throughout the city. Prices for bus tickets vary depending on the length of the journey, with single fares typically starting at around €1.50.

Regional Trains

For travelers looking to explore beyond the city limits, Pisa's regional train network offers convenient connections to nearby towns and attractions, including Florence, Lucca, and Cinque Terre. Managed by Trenitalia, Italy's national railway company, regional trains depart regularly from Pisa Centrale railway station, providing an efficient way to explore the surrounding region. Tickets for regional trains can be purchased at the station ticket office or online through the Trenitalia website, with prices varying depending on the destination and time of travel.

Bike Sharing

For eco-conscious travelers and fitness enthusiasts, Pisa offers a bike-sharing program that allows visitors to explore the city on two wheels. Managed by Mobike, the bike-sharing scheme provides access to a network of bicycles stationed at various locations throughout Pisa. Users can simply download the Mobike app, locate a bike using the built-in GPS system, and unlock it with their smartphone. Prices for bike rentals are typically based on usage time, with hourly rates starting at around €1.

Taxi Services

For travelers seeking a more convenient and personalized mode of transportation, taxi services are readily available in Pisa. Taxis can be hailed on the street or booked in advance through local taxi companies. While taxis offer door-to-door service and are ideal for short journeys or late-night travel, they tend to be more expensive than public transport options. Visitors should be aware that taxi fares in Pisa are regulated by law, with rates determined by the distance traveled and time of day.

From the convenient People Mover to the extensive bus network and regional train services, navigating Pisa's public transport networks is both easy and affordable. Whether you're exploring the city's historic center, venturing into the surrounding countryside, or embarking on day trips to nearby towns, Pisa's public transport options provide convenient access to all the attractions and landmarks the region has to offer. So hop on a bus, catch a train, or pedal your way through the city on a bike – the possibilities for exploration are endless in Pisa's vibrant and dynamic public transport network.

3.2 Taxis and Ride-Sharing Services

While exploring the enchanting city of Pisa, visitors often find themselves in need of convenient and efficient transportation options to navigate the streets and reach their destinations. Taxis and ride-sharing services offer travelers a flexible and personalized way to move around the city, providing door-to-door service and the convenience of on-demand transportation. Let's delve into the details of taxis and ride-sharing services in Pisa to help you make informed choices during your visit.

Traditional Taxis

Traditional taxis are readily available throughout Pisa, offering visitors a convenient mode of transportation for short journeys or late-night travel. Easily recognizable by their distinctive yellow color and rooftop taxi signs, licensed taxis can be hailed on the street or found at designated taxi ranks located at popular tourist spots, transportation hubs, and major landmarks. Taxi fares in Pisa are regulated by law and are determined by a combination of distance traveled and time of day. As of writing, the starting fare for a taxi ride in Pisa is around €5, with additional charges for distance and waiting time.

Taxi Companies

Several taxi companies operate in Pisa, providing a fleet of vehicles and professional drivers to meet the city's transportation needs. These companies offer a range of services, including airport transfers, city tours, and special event transportation. Some well-known taxi companies in Pisa include Cooperativa Pisana Autotaxi and Taxi Pisa 050, both of which have a reputation for reliability, safety, and excellent customer service. Visitors can easily book a taxi by phone, through the company's website, or by using a dedicated taxi app.

Ride-Sharing Services

In addition to traditional taxis, ride-sharing services have become increasingly popular in Pisa, offering travelers a convenient and cost-effective alternative for getting around the city. Companies like Uber and Lyft operate in Pisa, providing users with access to a network of private drivers who offer rides at competitive prices. Using a ride-sharing app, visitors can request a ride, track their driver's location in real-time, and pay for their journey electronically. Ride-sharing services often offer a range of vehicle options, including standard cars, luxury vehicles, and larger vehicles for groups or families.

Cost and Pricing

The cost of taxi rides and ride-sharing services in Pisa can vary depending on factors such as distance traveled, time of day, and demand. While taxis typically charge a base fare plus a rate per kilometer or minute of travel, ride-sharing services may use dynamic pricing algorithms that adjust fares based on supply and demand. As a general guideline, visitors can expect to pay between €1.50 to €2.50 per kilometer for taxi rides in Pisa, with additional charges for waiting time or luggage handling. Ride-sharing services may offer similar pricing structures, with fares calculated based on distance and time traveled.

Unique Features

Both taxis and ride-sharing services in Pisa offer unique features and benefits to travelers. Taxis provide the convenience of immediate access to transportation, with drivers who are familiar with the city's streets and attractions. Ride-sharing services, on the other hand, offer the flexibility of scheduling rides in advance, choosing preferred vehicle types, and paying electronically through the app. Additionally, ride-sharing apps often provide users with detailed information about their driver, including their name, photo, and vehicle details, enhancing safety and peace of mind.

Whether you opt for a traditional taxi or a ride-sharing service, navigating Pisa's streets is a breeze with these convenient transportation options at your disposal. From door-to-door service and flexible scheduling to competitive pricing and user-friendly apps, taxis and ride-sharing services offer visitors the freedom and convenience to explore the city at their own pace. So whether you're heading to the airport, touring the city's landmarks, or enjoying a night out on the town, taxis and ride-sharing services in Pisa provide a reliable and efficient means of getting around during your visit.

3.3 Renting a Car or Bike

When it comes to exploring the charming city of Pisa and its surrounding areas, renting a car or bike can offer visitors unparalleled freedom and flexibility. With the ability to venture off the beaten path and discover hidden gems at your own pace, renting a car or bike provides an exciting opportunity to explore Pisa and its picturesque countryside on your terms. Let's delve into the details of renting a car or bike in Pisa to help you make the most of your adventure.

Renting a Car

Renting a car in Pisa is a popular choice for travelers who want to explore the region's diverse landscapes and attractions at their own pace. Several well-known car rental companies operate in Pisa, offering a wide range of vehicles to suit every budget and preference. From compact cars and sedans to SUVs and luxury vehicles, visitors can choose the perfect car for their needs and embark on unforgettable road trips through Tuscany's rolling hills, vineyards, and medieval villages.

Cost and Pricing

The cost of renting a car in Pisa can vary depending on factors such as vehicle type, rental duration, and insurance coverage. As a general guideline, visitors can expect to pay anywhere from €30 to €100 per day for car rentals in Pisa, with additional fees for extras such as GPS navigation systems, child seats, and additional drivers. It's crucial to compare prices from various rental companies and carefully review the details to ensure you're getting the most favorable deal and comprehending the terms and conditions of your rental agreement.

Unique Features

Renting a car in Pisa offers travelers the freedom to explore the city and its surrounding areas at their own pace, without having to rely on public transportation schedules or tour operators. With a rental car, visitors can easily access remote attractions, scenic viewpoints, and charming villages that may be difficult to reach by other means. Additionally, rental cars often come equipped with modern amenities such as GPS navigation systems, air conditioning, and Bluetooth connectivity, making for a comfortable and enjoyable driving experience.

Renting a Bike

For eco-conscious travelers and fitness enthusiasts, renting a bike in Pisa provides an exciting opportunity to explore the city's historic streets and scenic waterfronts on two wheels. Several bike rental shops operate in Pisa, offering a variety of bicycles for rent, including city bikes, mountain bikes, and electric bikes. With dedicated bike lanes and paths throughout the city, Pisa is a bike-friendly destination that allows visitors to pedal their way through its charming neighborhoods and iconic landmarks with ease.

Cost and Pricing

The cost of renting a bike in Pisa is generally more affordable than renting a car, with prices starting at around €10 to €20 per day for standard bikes and €20 to €30 per day for electric bikes. Some bike rental shops may also offer hourly rates or discounted rates for longer rental periods. In addition to the rental fee, visitors may be required to leave a deposit or provide identification as security. It's advisable to inquire about insurance coverage and safety equipment such as helmets and locks when renting a bike.

Unique Features

Renting a bike in Pisa offers travelers a fun and eco-friendly way to explore the city's many attractions and landmarks. With its flat terrain and well-maintained bike paths, Pisa is ideally suited for cycling, allowing visitors to pedal their way from the iconic Leaning Tower to the picturesque Arno River waterfront and beyond. Many bike rental shops also provide maps, route suggestions, and insider tips to help visitors make the most of their cycling adventure in Pisa.

Whether you choose to rent a car and embark on scenic road trips through the Tuscan countryside or rent a bike and pedal your way through Pisa's historic streets, renting a car or bike offers travelers a convenient and enjoyable way to explore the city and its surroundings. With a wide range of vehicles and bicycles available for rent, as well as affordable pricing and unique features, renting a car or bike in Pisa provides visitors with the freedom and flexibility to create unforgettable memories during their stay. So why wait? Rent a car or bike in Pisa and embark on an adventure of a lifetime in this enchanting destination.

3.4 Walking Tours and Guided Transportation

Exploring the historic city of Pisa is an enriching experience, filled with iconic landmarks, charming streets, and fascinating history. To truly immerse yourself in the culture and heritage of Pisa, consider embarking on a walking tour or guided transportation adventure. These guided experiences offer visitors the opportunity to discover hidden gems, learn intriguing stories, and gain valuable insights into this captivating city.

Walking Tours

Walking tours are a popular way to explore Pisa's historic center, allowing visitors to stroll through cobblestone streets, admire architectural wonders, and soak in the vibrant atmosphere of the city. Led by knowledgeable guides, walking tours typically cover key attractions such as the Leaning Tower, Piazza dei Miracoli, Pisa Cathedral, and Piazza dei Cavalieri. Along the way, guides share fascinating anecdotes, historical facts, and insider tips, providing participants with a deeper understanding of Pisa's rich cultural heritage. Walking tours are suitable for travelers of all ages and fitness levels, offering a leisurely pace and ample opportunities for rest and photo stops.

Guided Transportation

For visitors seeking a more convenient and comprehensive way to explore Pisa and its surroundings, guided transportation tours offer an excellent option. These tours often include transportation by bus, minivan, or boat, allowing participants to cover more ground and visit off-the-beaten-path destinations beyond the city center. Guided transportation tours may include visits to nearby attractions such as the Tuscan countryside, charming villages, or coastal towns, providing travelers with a diverse and immersive experience of the region. With expert guides at the helm, participants can sit back, relax, and enjoy the journey while learning about the history, culture, and natural beauty of Pisa and its surroundings.

Private Tours

For a personalized and intimate experience, consider booking a private walking tour or guided transportation tour in Pisa. Private tours offer the flexibility to customize the itinerary according to your interests, preferences, and schedule, allowing you to explore Pisa at your own pace and focus on specific areas of interest. Whether you're interested in art and architecture, food and wine, or local culture and traditions, private tours can be tailored to suit your needs, ensuring a memorable and enriching experience tailored to your preferences.

Group Tours

Alternatively, group walking tours and guided transportation tours offer the opportunity to connect with fellow travelers and share the experience of exploring Pisa together. Joining a group tour allows participants to benefit from the expertise of a knowledgeable guide while enjoying the camaraderie of like-minded individuals. Group tours often provide a cost-effective option for budget-conscious travelers, with shared transportation and group discounts available for larger parties. Whether you're traveling solo, with family, or with friends, group tours offer a fun and social way to discover Pisa and create lasting memories with fellow adventurers.

Booking Information

To book a walking tour or guided transportation tour in Pisa, it's recommended to make reservations in advance, especially during peak tourist seasons. Many tour operators and travel agencies offer a variety of tour options, including different durations, themes, and languages. Visitors can research tour options online, read reviews from other travelers, and compare prices and itineraries to find the best fit for their needs. Additionally, some hotels and accommodations may offer tour booking services or recommendations for reputable tour operators in the area. Be sure to check the meeting point, departure times, and any inclusions or exclusions before booking to ensure a seamless and enjoyable experience.

Whether you prefer exploring on foot or embarking on a guided transportation adventure, walking tours and guided tours offer visitors a fantastic way to discover the beauty, history, and culture of Pisa. From iconic landmarks to hidden gems, these guided experiences provide valuable insights and memorable encounters that will enrich your visit to this enchanting city. So lace up your walking shoes, hop aboard a guided tour, and prepare to be captivated by the wonders of Pisa and its surroundings.

3.5 Accessibility Considerations for Travelers

Traveling to a new destination should be an enriching and inclusive experience for all visitors, regardless of their physical abilities. In Pisa, as in many other cities around the world, accessibility considerations play a crucial role in ensuring that travelers with disabilities can fully enjoy the sights, sounds, and experiences that the city has to offer. From transportation options to tourist attractions and accommodations, it's essential for travelers to be aware of accessibility considerations in Pisa to plan a comfortable and enjoyable trip.

Transportation Accessibility

When it comes to navigating Pisa's public transportation system, travelers with disabilities will find that certain options are more accessible than others. For example, the Pisa People Mover, which connects Pisa Centrale railway station with the city center, is equipped with ramps and elevators to accommodate passengers with mobility impairments. Similarly, some local buses in Pisa are equipped with low floors and wheelchair ramps, making them accessible to wheelchair users and travelers with limited mobility. However, it's important to note that not all buses may be fully accessible, so it's advisable to check with the transportation provider in advance.

Attractions and Landmarks

Many of Pisa's iconic attractions and landmarks, such as the Leaning Tower, Pisa Cathedral, and Piazza dei Miracoli, have made efforts to improve accessibility for visitors with disabilities. These sites often offer accessible entrances, ramps, and elevators to facilitate access for wheelchair users and travelers with mobility impairments. Additionally, some attractions may provide guided tours or audio guides with descriptive information for visitors with visual impairments. While accessibility features vary from site to site, most major tourist attractions in Pisa strive to ensure that all visitors can enjoy their visit regardless of their physical abilities.

Accommodations and Hotels

When choosing accommodations in Pisa, travelers with disabilities should consider factors such as wheelchair accessibility, bathroom facilities, and the availability of accessible rooms. Many hotels and guesthouses in Pisa offer accessible rooms with features such as widened doorways, roll-in showers, and grab bars to accommodate guests with mobility impairments. It's advisable to contact the accommodation directly to inquire about specific accessibility features and ensure that your needs can be met during your stay.

Dining and Entertainment

Pisa's dining and entertainment establishments vary in terms of accessibility, with some restaurants, cafes, and bars offering accessible entrances and facilities, while others may have limitations. When planning meals or entertainment options in Pisa, travelers with disabilities may want to research accessible venues in advance or contact establishments directly to inquire about accessibility features. Additionally, many tourist areas in Pisa are pedestrian-friendly, making it easier for travelers with mobility impairments to explore on foot.

Accessible Information and Resources

Travelers with disabilities visiting Pisa can benefit from accessible information and resources provided by local tourism authorities and organizations. Many tourist offices and websites offer information on accessible attractions, transportation options, and accommodations in Pisa, helping travelers plan their trip with confidence. Additionally, accessible travel guides and mobile apps may provide valuable insights and recommendations for navigating the city with ease.

Ensuring inclusivity and accessibility for all travelers is essential to creating a welcoming and enriching travel experience in Pisa. By considering accessibility considerations when planning transportation, accommodations, attractions, and dining options, travelers with disabilities can enjoy a comfortable and enjoyable visit to this historic city. With efforts to improve accessibility continuously underway, Pisa strives to be a destination where all visitors can explore, discover, and create lasting memories regardless of their physical abilities.

CHAPTER 4

TOP ATTRACTIONS/HIDDEN GEMS

Click the link or Scan QR Code with a device to view a comprehensive map of Top Attractions in Pisa – https://shorturl.at/bzHX8

4.1 The Leaning Tower of Pisa

Standing proudly in the heart of Pisa, Italy, the Leaning Tower of Pisa is arguably one of the most renowned and recognizable landmarks globally. Renowned for its distinctive tilt, this architectural marvel has captured the imagination of visitors for centuries, drawing millions of tourists from around the globe to marvel at its unique beauty and engineering ingenuity. Let's delve into the fascinating history, captivating architecture, and visitor experience of the Leaning Tower of Pisa.

Historical Significance

The Leaning Tower of Pisa, originally intended to be a freestanding bell tower for the adjacent Pisa Cathedral, began construction in the 12th century. However, the tower's gradual tilt began during its construction due to unstable soil and a poorly laid foundation. Despite efforts to correct the lean, including adjustments to subsequent floors, the tower continued to tilt over the centuries, eventually becoming a symbol of architectural imperfection and resilience.

Architectural Features

The Leaning Tower of Pisa is a remarkable example of Romanesque architecture, characterized by its round arches, decorative columns, and intricate carvings. Standing at approximately 56 meters (183 feet) tall, the tower consists of eight stories, including the chamber housing the bells at the top. The tilt of the tower is approximately 3.97 degrees off the vertical axis, creating a visually striking and somewhat surreal appearance that has captivated visitors for generations.

Visitor Experience

Visitors to the Leaning Tower of Pisa can embark on a journey of discovery as they explore this iconic landmark and its surrounding complex. Climbing the tower's spiral staircase offers breathtaking views of the cityscape and the chance to experience the tower's unique lean firsthand. Along the way, visitors can marvel at the intricate architectural details of the tower's interior, including the ornate marble columns and beautifully crafted arches.

Preservation Efforts

In recent years, efforts to preserve and stabilize the Leaning Tower of Pisa have been undertaken to ensure its longevity and safety for future generations. These efforts have included extensive restoration work, including the installation of counterweights and soil removal to reduce the tower's lean and prevent further subsidence. Notwithstanding the steps taken, the tower maintains its tilt, albeit with a slower inclination, highlighting the resilience of humanity and the timeless allure of this iconic landmark.

Visitor Tips

When arranging a trip to the Leaning Tower of Pisa, it's recommended to reserve tickets ahead of time, particularly during busy tourist periods, to skip lengthy queues and guarantee availability. Visitors should also be prepared for a moderate physical challenge when climbing the tower's spiral staircase, as the narrow steps and uneven incline can be demanding. Additionally, photography enthusiasts will want to capture the tower from various angles and perspectives to fully appreciate its unique tilt and architectural splendor.

The Leaning Tower of Pisa stands as a timeless symbol of human ingenuity, resilience, and the enduring allure of architectural marvels. From its intriguing history and captivating architecture to its breathtaking views and visitor experience, the tower continues to captivate the hearts and minds of travelers from around the world. Whether you're marveling at its lean from afar or climbing its spiral staircase for a closer look, a visit to the Leaning Tower of Pisa is sure to leave a lasting impression and create cherished memories for years to come.

4.2 Piazza dei Miracoli (Square of Miracles)

Nestled in the heart of Pisa, Italy, the Piazza dei Miracoli, also known as the Square of Miracles, is a breathtaking architectural ensemble that has captivated visitors for centuries. This UNESCO World Heritage Site is renowned for its stunning collection of medieval buildings, including the iconic Leaning Tower of Pisa, making it one of Italy's most visited attractions. Let's explore the rich history, magnificent architecture, and visitor experience of the Piazza dei Miracoli.

Historical Significance

The history of the Piazza dei Miracoli dates back to the 11th century when construction began on the Pisa Cathedral, the centerpiece of the square. Over the following centuries, additional structures were added to the square, including the Leaning Tower of Pisa, the Baptistery of St. John, and the Camposanto Monumentale (Monumental Cemetery). The square's name, "Piazza dei Miracoli," or Square of Miracles, is believed to have originated from a 17th-century Italian poet who described the area as a miraculous sight.

Architectural Splendor

The Piazza dei Miracoli is a testament to the exquisite craftsmanship and architectural genius of medieval Italy. The highlight of the square is undoubtedly the Pisa Cathedral, a masterpiece of Romanesque architecture adorned with intricate facades, elegant arches, and stunning marble columns. The Baptistery of St. John, renowned for its unique circular design and ornate decorations, stands adjacent to the cathedral, while the Camposanto Monumentale features a striking Gothic facade and houses a collection of ancient Roman sarcophagi and frescoes.

Visitor Experience

A visit to the Piazza dei Miracoli offers a truly immersive experience into the rich history and cultural heritage of Pisa. Visitors can wander through the square's open expanse, marveling at the majestic architecture and taking in the serene atmosphere. Climbing the Leaning Tower of Pisa provides a unique perspective of the square and offers panoramic views of the surrounding cityscape. Inside the cathedral and baptistery, visitors can admire the intricate mosaics, frescoes, and sculptures that adorn these sacred spaces, while the Camposanto Monumentale provides a tranquil retreat for contemplation and reflection.

Preservation and Restoration

In recent years, efforts have been made to preserve and restore the architectural treasures of the Piazza dei Miracoli, ensuring their longevity for future generations to enjoy. Conservation projects have included structural stabilization, cleaning and restoration of facades, and the implementation of measures to mitigate the impact of tourism on the delicate marble structures. These efforts aim to safeguard the square's architectural heritage while maintaining its integrity and authenticity as a cultural landmark.

Visitor Tips

When planning a visit to the Piazza dei Miracoli, it's advisable to arrive early or late in the day to avoid the crowds and enjoy a more peaceful experience. Visitors should also purchase tickets in advance for attractions such as the Leaning Tower of Pisa, as availability may be limited, especially during peak tourist seasons. Additionally, comfortable walking shoes and sun protection are recommended, as exploring the square and its surrounding attractions may involve considerable walking and exposure to the sun.

The Piazza dei Miracoli stands as a testament to the artistic and architectural achievements of medieval Italy, drawing visitors from around the world to marvel at its magnificent beauty and historical significance. Whether admiring the graceful curves of the Leaning Tower, gazing up at the celestial dome of the cathedral, or wandering through the tranquil cloisters of the Camposanto Monumentale, a visit to the Square of Miracles is a truly unforgettable experience that will leave a lasting impression on all who have the privilege to behold its splendor.

4.3 Museums and Galleries

Pisa isn't just about its iconic leaning tower and historic cathedral; it's also home to a rich cultural heritage preserved within its museums and galleries. Here are five must-visit establishments where you can delve into the art, history, and science of this enchanting city.

1. Museo Nazionale di San Matteo (National Museum of San Matteo)

Just a stone's throw away from the Leaning Tower, the Museo Nazionale di San Matteo is housed in a former Benedictine convent. This museum showcases an impressive collection of medieval and Renaissance art, including sculptures, paintings, and decorative arts. Visitors can admire works by renowned artists such as Simone Martini, Masaccio, and Francesco Traini. The museum is open from Tuesday to Sunday, from 10:00 AM to 6:00 PM. Admission fees vary but generally range from €5 to €10, with discounts available for students and seniors.

2. Palazzo Blu

Situated along the picturesque Lungarno Gambacorti, Palazzo Blu is a vibrant cultural center that hosts temporary exhibitions and cultural events throughout the year. Housed in a beautifully restored historic palace, the gallery showcases a diverse range of contemporary art, photography, and multimedia installations. In addition to its exhibition spaces, Palazzo Blu also features a cafe, bookstore, and outdoor terrace overlooking the Arno River. Opening hours vary depending on the current exhibition, so it's best to check the official website for up-to-date information. Admission prices typically range from €8 to €12 for adults, with discounts available for children and seniors.

3. Museo delle Sinopie (Sinopie Museum)

Located adjacent to the Leaning Tower in the Campo dei Miracoli, the museum is located in the former hospital of Santa Chiara and exhibits a distinctive collection of sinopias.which are preparatory drawings and sketches created by Renaissance artists before executing frescoes. Visitors can learn about the process of fresco painting and observe the intricate details of these preliminary artworks. The Sinopie Museum is open daily, with operating hours typically from 9:00 AM to 8:00 PM during the summer months and from 9:00 AM to 6:00 PM during the winter months. Admission fees range from €5 to €8, with discounts available for students and groups.

4. Museo dell'Opera del Duomo (Opera del Duomo Museum)

The Museo dell'Opera del Duomo is dedicated to the history and art of Pisa's iconic cathedral complex. Situated near the Piazza dei Miracoli, the museum houses an extensive collection of sculptures, artifacts, and architectural fragments dating back to the medieval period. Highlights include masterpieces by Nicola Pisano, Giovanni Pisano, and Donatello, as well as a scale model of the cathedral complex. The museum is open daily, with hours of operation typically from 10:00 AM to 6:00 PM. Admission prices range from €5 to €8, with discounts available for children and seniors.

5. Museo di Storia Naturale e del Territorio (Museum of Natural History and Territory)

The Museo di Storia Naturale e del Territorio offers a fascinating journey through the natural history and geological heritage of the Pisa region. Located within the historic Palazzo Lanfranchi, the museum's exhibits cover a wide range of topics, including geology, paleontology, botany, and zoology, with specimens ranging from fossils and minerals to taxidermy animals and botanical collections. The museum is open from Tuesday to Sunday, with hours of operation typically from 9:00 AM to 7:00 PM. Admission fees vary but generally range from €5 to €8 for adults, with discounts available for children and students.

From medieval art to contemporary exhibitions, Pisa's museums and galleries offer a diverse range of cultural experiences for visitors to explore. Whether you're interested in Renaissance masterpieces, contemporary art installations, or natural history exhibits, these five establishments provide enriching opportunities to delve into the rich cultural heritage of this historic city. Be sure to check opening hours, admission prices, and any special exhibitions before planning your visit to make the most of your museum-hopping adventure in Pisa!

4.4 Parks and Gardens

Pisa, with its rich cultural heritage and historic landmarks, also boasts a serene and green side with its array of beautiful parks and gardens. These natural getaways provide visitors with a peaceful break from the hustle and bustle of the city, providing opportunities for relaxation, recreation, and appreciation of nature's beauty. Here are enchanting parks and gardens in Pisa that are worth exploring:

1. Giardino Scotto (Scotto Garden)

Located along the banks of the Arno River, Giardino Scotto is a charming urban park that offers panoramic views of the river and the city skyline. The park features lush greenery, shaded pathways, and scenic viewpoints, making it an ideal spot for a leisurely stroll or a peaceful picnic. Visitors can also enjoy outdoor concerts, art exhibitions, and cultural events hosted in the park throughout the year. Giardino Scotto is open daily from dawn to dusk, providing ample opportunities to enjoy its natural beauty and scenic vistas.

2. Orto Botanico di Pisa (Botanical Garden of Pisa)

The Orto Botanico di Pisa is one of the oldest botanical gardens in Europe, dating back to the 16th century. This tranquil oasis is home to a diverse collection of plant species from around the world, including rare and exotic specimens. Visitors can wander through themed gardens, greenhouses, and outdoor exhibits, learning about the importance of plant conservation and biodiversity. Nestled within the historic center of

Pisa, the botanical garden is open to the public from Tuesday to Sunday, with hours of operation typically from 9:00 AM to 7:00 PM.

3. Parco Regionale Migliarino San Rossore Massaciuccoli (Migliarino San Rossore Massaciuccoli Regional Park)

Stretching along the coast of the Tyrrhenian Sea, the Migliarino San Rossore Massaciuccoli Regional Park is a vast natural reserve that encompasses diverse ecosystems, including forests, wetlands, and sand dunes. Visitors to the park can explore scenic hiking and biking trails, go birdwatching, or enjoy a leisurely picnic amidst the tranquil surroundings. The park is open year-round, with varying hours depending on the season, so it's advisable to check the official website for updated information before planning your visit.

4. Parco Naturale Migliarino-San Rossore-Massaciuccoli (Migliarino-San Rossore-Massaciuccoli Natural Park):

Another section of the larger regional park, the Migliarino-San Rossore-Massaciuccoli Natural Park, offers visitors the opportunity to immerse themselves in the beauty of the Tuscan countryside. The park is home to diverse flora and fauna, including Mediterranean scrubland, pine forests, and marshlands teeming with birdlife. Visitors can explore nature trails, go horseback riding, or take guided boat tours along the park's waterways. Opening hours vary depending on the area of the park and the activities available, so it's recommended to check ahead of time.

5. Parco di Villa Paganini (Villa Paganini Park)

Located in the outskirts of Pisa, Villa Paganini Park is a picturesque green space that offers a peaceful respite from the city center. The park features manicured lawns, towering trees, and meandering pathways, perfect for a leisurely stroll or a relaxing afternoon picnic. Visitors can also explore the historic villa, which dates back to the 18th century and serves as a cultural center hosting art exhibitions, concerts, and special events. Villa Paganini Park is open daily during daylight hours, providing a tranquil escape for nature lovers and outdoor enthusiasts alike.

6. Parco Naturale di Migliarino-San Rossore-Massaciuccoli (Natural Park of Migliarino-San Rossore-Massaciuccoli)

Situated between Pisa and the coastal town of Marina di Pisa, the Natural Park of Migliarino-San Rossore-Massaciuccoli is a pristine natural reserve that encompasses a mosaic of habitats, including pine forests, sand dunes, and wetlands. Visitors to the park can explore scenic hiking and biking trails, go birdwatching, or relax on the pristine beaches along the Mediterranean coast. The park is open year-round, with varying hours depending on the season and area of the park, so it's advisable to check ahead of time before planning your visit.

Whether you're seeking a peaceful stroll through manicured gardens, a scenic hike amidst pristine natural landscapes, or a cultural experience in a historic villa, Pisa's parks and gardens offer something for everyone to enjoy. From urban oases to expansive nature reserves, these green spaces provide opportunities for relaxation, recreation, and appreciation of the natural world. So take a break from sightseeing and immerse yourself in the beauty of Pisa's parks and gardens during your visit to this charming Italian city!

4.5 Hidden Gems: Off-the-Beaten-Path Discoveries

Click the link or Scan QR Code with a device to view a comprehensive map of Hidden Gems in Pisa – https://shorturl.at/asBN4

While Pisa is renowned for its iconic Leaning Tower and grandiose cathedral, there's much more to this historic city than meets the eye. Beyond the popular tourist routes lie hidden treasures waiting to be uncovered by adventurous travelers. From charming neighborhoods and local markets to lesser-known museums and scenic parks, these off-the-beaten-path destinations offer a glimpse into the authentic heart and soul of Pisa.

Exploring Charming Neighborhoods

Venture beyond the bustling tourist areas and immerse yourself in the authentic charm of Pisa's lesser-known neighborhoods. Wander through the narrow cobblestone streets of San Martino, where medieval architecture and quaint cafes beckon visitors to linger and explore. Stroll along the picturesque canals of Borgo Stretto, lined with colorful buildings and artisan shops offering handmade goods and local delicacies. In these hidden corners of Pisa, you'll find a treasure trove of authentic experiences waiting to be uncovered.

Discovering Local Markets

For a taste of everyday life in Pisa, venture into the city's vibrant local markets, where locals gather to shop for fresh produce, artisanal products, and unique souvenirs. The Mercato delle Vettovaglie, located near the Arno River, is a bustling market brimming with colorful stalls selling fruits, vegetables, cheeses, and other local specialties. Here, you can sample delicious Tuscan delicacies, chat with friendly vendors, and immerse yourself in the lively atmosphere of the market.

Hidden Museums and Galleries

Pisa is home to a wealth of museums and galleries beyond the well-known attractions of the Piazza dei Miracoli. Explore the Museo delle Sinopie, housed in the former hospital of Santa Chiara, which showcases preparatory sketches and drawings for the city's famous frescoes. Delve into the Museo Nazionale di San Matteo, tucked away in a former Benedictine convent, to admire its collection of medieval and Renaissance art. These hidden gems offer a deeper insight into Pisa's rich cultural heritage away from the crowds.

Tranquil Parks and Gardens

Escape the hustle and bustle of the city and seek solace in Pisa's tranquil parks and gardens. Explore the Orto Botanico, one of the oldest botanical gardens in Europe, where exotic plants and fragrant flowers flourish amidst serene greenery. Enjoying a leisurely walk through Giardino Scotto, a delightful park situated along the Arno River, where shady trees and blooming flowers provide a peaceful retreat from the urban landscape. These hidden oases offer a welcome respite for weary travelers seeking tranquility amidst the city's hustle and bustle.

Culinary Delights Off the Beaten Path
Indulge your taste buds in Pisa's lesser-known culinary delights, away from the tourist traps and crowded restaurants. Discover cozy trattorias tucked away in quiet alleys, where local chefs prepare traditional Tuscan dishes using fresh, seasonal ingredients sourced from nearby markets. Savor homemade pasta dishes, succulent meats, and decadent desserts, accompanied by fine wines from the region's renowned vineyards. In these hidden culinary gems, you'll experience the true flavors of Pisa in an authentic and unforgettable dining experience.

Connecting with Local Culture
Immerse yourself in the vibrant local culture of Pisa by attending off-the-beaten-path events and festivals that celebrate the city's traditions and heritage. From community festivals and craft markets to concerts featuring live music, there's always something happening beneath the surface of Pisa's tourist attractions. Engage with locals, learn about their customs and traditions, and forge meaningful connections that will enrich your travel experience and leave lasting memories of your time in Pisa.

While the Leaning Tower may be Pisa's most famous landmark, the city's hidden gems offer a deeper and more authentic glimpse into its rich history, culture, and way of life. From charming neighborhoods and local markets to hidden museums and tranquil parks, these off-the-beaten-path discoveries invite visitors to explore beyond the tourist trail and uncover the true essence of Pisa. So, venture off the beaten path, embrace serendipitous encounters, and let the hidden gems of Pisa reveal their secrets to you.

CHAPTER 5

PRACTICAL INFORMATION AND TRAVEL RESOURCES

5.1 Maps and Navigation

Click the link or Scan the QR Code with a device to view a comprehensive map of Pisa – https://shorturl.at/IL689

Exploring the picturesque city of Pisa is a delightful adventure, but navigating its charming streets and alleys can sometimes be daunting for first-time visitors. Fear not! With the right maps and navigation tools at your disposal, you'll be able to navigate Pisa's labyrinthine lanes with ease and discover its hidden treasures. From essential landmarks to hidden gems, shopping centers, and dining hotspots, this guide will equip you with everything you need to navigate Pisa like a seasoned traveler.

Essential Landmarks on the Toledo Tourist Map

The Toledo Tourist Map is an invaluable resource for navigating Pisa's city center. Essential landmarks such as the Leaning Tower of Pisa, Pisa Cathedral (Duomo di Pisa), and Baptistery of St. John (Battistero di San Giovanni) are prominently featured on the map, making it easy to orient yourself and plan your itinerary. Additionally, the map highlights other notable attractions like the Museo dell'Opera del Duomo, Museo Nazionale di San Matteo, and Palazzo Blu, ensuring you don't miss out on any of Pisa's cultural treasures.

Hotels and Accommodations

Finding the perfect place to stay in Pisa is made simple with the Toledo Tourist Map, which includes markers for various hotels and accommodations scattered throughout the city. From luxurious hotels like the Grand Hotel Duomo and Hotel Relais

Dell'Orologio to budget-friendly options such as Hotel La Pace and Hostel Pisa Tower, there's something to suit every traveler's preferences and budget. Use the map to locate your chosen accommodation and plan your route accordingly.

Hidden Gems and Off-the-Beaten-Path Discoveries
While the main tourist attractions are undoubtedly impressive, don't overlook Pisa's hidden gems tucked away in its lesser-known corners. The Toledo Tourist Map may not explicitly highlight these hidden treasures, but with a keen eye and a spirit of exploration, you can uncover charming neighborhoods, quaint cafes, artisanal shops, and tranquil parks that offer a glimpse into the authentic soul of Pisa. Keep an eye out for intriguing alleyways and side streets as you navigate the city—they often lead to delightful surprises.

Shopping Centers and Boutiques
Whether you're in search of designer fashion, artisanal crafts, or unique souvenirs, Pisa has a wealth of shopping options to suit every taste. The Toledo Tourist Map identifies key shopping centers and boutiques scattered throughout the city, including the Galleria Vittorio Emanuele II, Corso Italia, and Borgo Stretto. From high-end boutiques to quaint artisan workshops, these shopping destinations offer a diverse array of goods for discerning shoppers.

Dining and Nightlife Hotspots
After a day of sightseeing, indulge in Pisa's vibrant dining and nightlife scene, which boasts an array of restaurants, cafes, and bars to satisfy every palate. The Toledo Tourist Map highlights popular dining districts such as Piazza delle Vettovaglie and Piazza Garibaldi, where you can sample authentic Tuscan cuisine and sip on fine wines late into the night. Whether you're craving traditional Italian fare or international flavors, the map will guide you to the perfect spot for a memorable dining experience.

Navigation Tips and Directions

While the Toledo Tourist Map provides a helpful overview of Pisa's main attractions and landmarks, don't be afraid to explore beyond its borders. Keep a smartphone or physical map handy for navigating lesser-known areas and discovering hidden gems off the beaten path. Remember to wear comfortable walking shoes, as Pisa's narrow streets and uneven cobblestones can be challenging to navigate. Additionally, familiarize yourself with key landmarks and street names to help orient yourself as you explore the city.

Practical Information

When using the Toledo Tourist Map, it's essential to pay attention to scale and orientation to ensure accurate navigation. Familiarize yourself with common map symbols and legends to interpret the map effectively. Additionally, be mindful of opening hours for attractions, restaurants, and shops, as these may vary depending on the day of the week and the season. Lastly, don't hesitate to ask locals for directions or recommendations—they're often happy to share insider tips and hidden gems with curious travelers.

With its comprehensive coverage of essential landmarks, accommodations, dining hotspots, and more, the Toledo Tourist Map is an indispensable tool for navigating Pisa's enchanting streets and discovering its hidden treasures. Armed with this invaluable resource and a spirit of adventure, you'll be well-equipped to explore the city's rich cultural heritage, vibrant dining scene, and charming neighborhoods like a seasoned traveler. So grab your map, lace up your walking shoes, and embark on a memorable journey through the captivating city of Pisa!

5.2 Essential Packing List

Embarking on a journey to Pisa promises to be an unforgettable experience filled with historic landmarks, delicious cuisine, and charming streets waiting to be explored. To ensure you make the most of your trip, it's essential to pack wisely. Here's a detailed guide to help you pack everything you need for your visit to Pisa.

Clothing

Pisa's climate is generally mild, but it's wise to pack layers to accommodate any fluctuations in temperature. Lightweight, breathable fabrics are ideal for exploring the city comfortably. Don't forget to bring comfortable walking shoes for navigating Pisa's cobblestone streets and exploring its historic sites. If you plan to visit religious sites such as the cathedral, remember to pack modest clothing that covers your shoulders and knees.

Accessories

Sun protection is crucial, especially during the summer months, so be sure to pack sunglasses, a wide-brimmed hat, and sunscreen to shield yourself from the sun's rays. A compact umbrella or rain jacket is also handy for unexpected showers, which are not uncommon in Pisa, particularly in the spring and autumn months.

Electronics and Gadgets

Capture memories of your Pisa adventure with a camera or smartphone equipped with a good quality camera. Don't forget to bring chargers and adapters suitable for European outlets to keep your devices powered throughout your trip. A portable power bank can also be a lifesaver for long days of sightseeing.

Travel Documents

Ensure you have all necessary travel documents, including your passport, visa (if required), travel insurance, and any relevant reservations or confirmations for accommodations, tours, or transportation. It's a good idea to make photocopies or digital scans of these documents and store them securely in case of loss or theft.

Money and Payment Methods

Bring a mix of payment methods, including cash (in euros) for smaller purchases and credit/debit cards for larger expenses. Notify your bank of your travel plans to avoid any issues with card usage abroad. Consider carrying a money belt or secure wallet to keep your valuables safe while exploring crowded tourist areas.

Medical Supplies

Pack any essential medications, along with a small first aid kit containing basic supplies such as adhesive bandages, antiseptic wipes, pain relievers, and motion sickness medication if needed. Remember to bring any prescription medications in their original packaging with clear labels.

Travel Accessories

Invest in a sturdy, lightweight backpack or day bag to carry your essentials while exploring Pisa. A reusable water bottle is also handy for staying hydrated throughout the day, especially in warmer weather. Consider packing a pocket-sized guidebook or map to navigate the city without relying solely on digital devices.

Language Resources

While many locals in Pisa speak English, learning a few basic Italian phrases can enhance your travel experience and help you connect with locals. Consider packing a pocket-sized phrasebook or downloading a language app to assist with communication.

By packing thoughtfully and preparing for various aspects of your Pisa adventure, you can ensure a smooth and enjoyable travel experience. Remember to tailor your packing list to your individual needs and preferences, and don't forget to leave a little room in your suitcase for souvenirs and mementos of your time in this enchanting Italian city. With the right essentials on hand, you'll be ready to explore Pisa's iconic landmarks, savor its delicious cuisine, and create unforgettable memories that will last a lifetime.

5.3 Visa Requirements and Entry Procedures

Before embarking on your journey to Pisa, it's essential to familiarize yourself with the visa requirements based on your nationality. Italy, being a member of the Schengen Area, allows citizens of many countries to enter for short stays without obtaining a visa. Travelers from Schengen Area member states, as well as certain other countries, typically enjoy visa-free entry for stays of up to 90 days within a 180-day period.

However, it's crucial to check the specific visa requirements for your country of citizenship well in advance of your trip to ensure compliance.

Researching Visa Exemptions

Certain travelers may be exempt from the Schengen visa requirement based on their nationality or the purpose of their visit. For example, citizens of the European Union (EU) and European Free Trade Association (EFTA) member states, as well as citizens of certain other countries, may enjoy visa-free travel to Italy for short stays. Additionally, travelers visiting for purposes such as tourism, business meetings, or family visits may also be exempt from the visa requirement. Be sure to research whether you qualify for any visa exemptions based on your circumstances.

Applying for a Schengen Visa

If your country of citizenship is not exempt from the Schengen visa requirement, you'll need to apply for a Schengen visa through the Italian consulate or embassy in your home country. The application process typically involves completing a visa application form, providing supporting documents such as a valid passport, proof of travel insurance, proof of accommodation, and proof of sufficient financial means to cover your stay in Italy. Additionally, you may be required to attend an in-person interview as part of the visa application process.

Planning Your Itinerary

When applying for a Schengen visa, it's essential to have a clear itinerary outlining your intended travel dates, destinations, and accommodations in Italy. Your itinerary should demonstrate that you have a legitimate purpose for visiting Italy and that you intend to return to your home country before your visa expires. Be prepared to provide details of your planned activities in Pisa and any other cities you plan to visit during your stay.

Entry Procedures and Border Control

Upon arrival in Pisa, travelers are required to go through passport control and border checks, even if they hold a valid Schengen visa. Make sure to have all necessary documents readily accessible, including your passport, visa (if applicable), and any supporting documents you provided during the visa application process. Be prepared to answer questions from border control officers about the purpose of your visit, your accommodations, and your planned activities during your stay in Pisa.

Staying Informed

Visa requirements and entry procedures can vary depending on your country of citizenship, so it's essential to stay informed about any updates or changes to the regulations. Check the website of the Italian consulate or embassy in your home country for the most up-to-date information on visa requirements and application procedures. Additionally, consider enrolling in your country's travel advisory program to receive alerts and updates about travel advisories and security alerts related to Italy.

Navigating visa requirements and entry procedures can seem daunting, but with careful planning and preparation, you can ensure a smooth and hassle-free journey to Pisa. Whether you're eligible for visa-free travel or need to apply for a Schengen visa, be sure to research the requirements well in advance of your trip and gather all necessary documents to support your application. By staying informed and following the guidelines provided by the Italian authorities, you'll be well-equipped to enjoy your visit to Pisa with peace of mind.

5.4 Safety Tips and Emergency Contacts

When visiting Pisa, it's important to be aware of the local safety considerations to ensure a smooth and enjoyable experience. While Pisa is generally a safe destination for tourists, it's always wise to exercise caution and be mindful of your surroundings, especially in crowded tourist areas where pickpocketing and petty theft may occur. Stay alert and keep your belongings secure to minimize the risk of theft or loss.

Navigating the City Safely

As you explore Pisa's charming streets and landmarks, take care when crossing busy roads and intersections, and adhere to traffic signals and pedestrian crossings.

Sidewalks may be narrow and uneven in some areas, so watch your step to avoid tripping or stumbling. If you plan to use public transportation, be cautious when boarding buses or trains, and keep an eye on your belongings at all times.

Emergency Contacts and Assistance

In the event of an emergency or if you require assistance during your visit to Pisa, it's essential to know who to contact for help. The universal emergency number in Italy is 112, which connects you to police, ambulance, and fire services. If you need non-emergency assistance, you can contact the local police station (Questura) or Carabinieri station for help and guidance. Additionally, your country's embassy or consulate in Italy can provide support and assistance to citizens in need.

Health and Medical Services

Should you require medical assistance during your stay in Pisa, rest assured that the city is equipped with hospitals, clinics, and pharmacies to cater to your needs. In case of a medical emergency, dial 118 to request an ambulance, or visit the nearest hospital emergency department for immediate care. It's advisable to carry travel insurance that covers medical expenses and emergency evacuation to ensure you receive prompt and comprehensive medical care if needed.

Staying Informed and Vigilant

Stay informed about local safety advisories, weather alerts, and any potential risks or hazards that may affect your visit to Pisa. Check with your accommodation or local authorities for updates on safety conditions and any specific precautions you should take. Remain vigilant and trust your instincts—if something doesn't feel right, err on the side of caution and remove yourself from the situation.

Cultural Sensitivity and Respect

While safety concerns may vary from person to person, it's essential to also consider cultural sensitivities and show respect for local customs and traditions during your visit to Pisa. Dress modestly when visiting religious sites such as the Pisa Cathedral, and be mindful of local customs regarding greetings, gestures, and social interactions. By showing respect for the local culture and customs, you'll enhance your safety and foster positive interactions with the people of Pisa.

By following these safety tips and being prepared for emergencies, you can enjoy a safe and memorable visit to Pisa. Stay vigilant, keep your belongings secure, and familiarize yourself with emergency contacts and procedures to ensure peace of mind throughout your journey. With a bit of caution and preparedness, you'll be able to explore Pisa's enchanting streets and landmarks with confidence and security.

5.5 Currency, Banking, Budgeting and Money Matters

When planning your visit to Pisa, it's essential to familiarize yourself with the local currency. Italy's official currency is the Euro (€), which is divided into coins (cents) and banknotes. Euros are widely accepted throughout Pisa, from restaurants and shops to tourist attractions and transportation services. It's a good idea to carry a mix of cash and cards for convenience and flexibility during your stay.

Exchanging Currency

If you need to exchange currency upon arrival in Pisa, you'll find currency exchange offices (cambio) at airports, train stations, and major tourist areas. While these establishments offer convenience, they may charge higher exchange rates and fees compared to banks. Alternatively, you can withdraw Euros directly from ATMs using your debit or credit card, which often provides a more favorable exchange rate.

Banking Services and ATMs

Pisa is equipped with a network of banks and ATMs where you can access banking services and withdraw cash as needed. Major banks such as UniCredit, Intesa Sanpaolo, and Banca Monte dei Paschi di Siena have branches located throughout the city, offering a range of services including currency exchange, cash withdrawals, and account management. ATMs are also widely available and accept most major international cards.

Budgeting for Your Trip

Before setting off on your Pisa adventure, it's wise to establish a travel budget to help manage your expenses effectively. Consider factors such as accommodation costs, dining expenses, transportation fares, entrance fees to attractions, and souvenirs. Research average prices for meals, accommodations, and activities in Pisa to gauge how much you'll need to budget for each day of your stay.

Paying for Goods and Services

In Pisa, credit and debit cards are widely accepted at most establishments, including restaurants, hotels, shops, and tourist attractions. Visa and Mastercard are the most commonly accepted card networks, although some smaller establishments may only accept cash. It's a good idea to carry a small amount of cash for purchases at local markets or small vendors who may not accept cards.

Tips for Using Cards Abroad

When using your debit or credit card in Pisa, be mindful of potential fees associated with foreign transactions, currency conversion, and ATM withdrawals. Check with your bank or card issuer beforehand to understand any applicable fees and charges. Additionally, inform your bank of your travel plans to avoid any issues with card usage abroad, such as security blocks or fraud alerts.

Safety and Security Measures

To safeguard your finances while traveling in Pisa, take precautions such as keeping your cards and cash secure, avoiding carrying large sums of money, and using ATMs located in well-lit, secure areas. Be vigilant against card skimming devices and only use ATMs affiliated with reputable banks. Consider using a money belt or hidden wallet to store valuables discreetly while exploring the city.

By understanding the currency, banking services, and money matters in Pisa, you can navigate financial transactions with confidence and ease during your visit. Whether you're exchanging currency, withdrawing cash, or using cards for purchases, being informed about local practices and potential fees will help you make the most of your travel budget and enjoy a seamless experience in the charming city of Pisa.

5.6 Language, Communication and Useful Phrases

While Italian is the official language spoken in Pisa, many locals, especially those working in the tourism industry, also speak English, making it relatively easy for English-speaking visitors to communicate. However, learning a few basic Italian phrases can enhance your experience and demonstrate respect for the local culture.

Essential Phrases for Communication

Before your trip to Pisa, consider learning or familiarizing yourself with some essential Italian phrases to help you navigate daily interactions. Here are a few useful phrases to get you started:

- Buongiorno (BWON-johr-noh)** - Good morning
- Buonasera (BWOH-nah-SEH-rah)** - Good evening
- Grazie (GRAH-tsyeh)** - Thank you
- Per favore (pehr fah-VOH-reh)** - Please
- Scusa (SKOO-zah)** - Excuse me / Sorry
- Parla inglese? (PAHR-lah een-GLEH-zeh)** - Do you speak English?
- Dove si trova...? (DOH-veh see TROH-vah)** - Where is...?

Navigating Language Barriers

If you encounter language barriers during your visit to Pisa, don't be discouraged. Most locals are friendly and accommodating, and they will appreciate your efforts to communicate in Italian, even if it's just a few basic phrases. Consider using gestures, pointing, and simple English words to convey your message if needed.

Utilizing Translation Apps

To aid communication and overcome language barriers, consider downloading translation apps such as Google Translate or Duolingo before your trip. These apps allow you to translate text, speech, and even images in real-time, making it easier to communicate with locals and understand signs, menus, and other written text in Italian.

Seeking Assistance

If you find yourself in need of assistance or directions during your stay in Pisa, don't hesitate to ask for help. Locals are generally friendly and approachable, and they will often go out of their way to assist visitors. Whether you need directions to a specific landmark or recommendations for a good restaurant, don't be afraid to ask for help.

Learning About Local Customs

In addition to language, familiarize yourself with local customs and etiquette to ensure respectful interactions with locals. For example, it's customary to greet people with a friendly "Buongiorno" or "Buonasera" when entering a shop or restaurant. Additionally, remember to use "Grazie" (thank you) when receiving assistance or service.

By embracing the local language, communicating respectfully, and learning a few useful phrases, you can enhance your experience and forge meaningful connections with the people of Pisa. Whether you're ordering a cappuccino at a cafe, asking for directions to the Leaning Tower, or simply greeting locals with a friendly "Buongiorno," your efforts to engage with the local culture will enrich your visit and leave you with lasting memories of your time in this charming Italian city.

5.7 Useful Websites, Mobile Apps and Online Resources

Before embarking on your journey to Pisa, it's beneficial to familiarize yourself with a variety of online resources that can enhance your travel experience. Websites such as Visit Tuscany (https://www.visittuscany.com/) provide comprehensive information about Pisa's attractions, events, and local culture. Additionally, the official website of the Pisa Tourism Board (https://www.turismo.pisa.it/en/) offers valuable insights into accommodations, dining options, and transportation services in the city.

Harnessing the Power of Mobile Apps

Mobile apps can be invaluable tools for navigating Pisa's bustling streets and discovering hidden gems. Citymapper (https://citymapper.com/) is a popular app that offers real-time transit information, including bus and train schedules, route planning, and fare estimates. Google Maps (https://www.google.com/maps) is another essential app that provides detailed maps, directions, and reviews for attractions, restaurants, and hotels in Pisa.

Booking Accommodations with Ease

When it comes to booking accommodations in Pisa, online booking platforms such as Booking.com (https://www.booking.com/) and Airbnb (https://www.airbnb.com/)provide a diverse array of choices to accommodate every budget and preference whether you're seeking a luxurious hotel room with a view of the Leaning Tower or a cozy apartment in the heart of the city, these platforms make it easy to find the perfect place to stay.

Discovering Local Experiences

To uncover authentic local experiences and activities in Pisa, consider browsing platforms such as Viator (https://www.viator.com/) and GetYourGuide (https://www.getyourguide.com/). These websites offer a plethora of guided tours, excursions, and cultural experiences led by knowledgeable local guides. Whether you're interested in a guided walking tour of Pisa's historic center or a wine tasting experience in the Tuscan countryside, these platforms have something for every traveler.

Staying Connected with Travel Communities

Joining online travel communities and forums can provide valuable insights and recommendations from fellow travelers who have explored Pisa before you. Websites such as TripAdvisor (https://www.tripadvisor.com/) and Lonely Planet's Thorn Tree forum (https://www.lonelyplanet.com/thorntree) are excellent resources for seeking advice, sharing experiences, and connecting with like-minded travelers. You can also follow social media accounts and hashtags related to Pisa to stay updated on the latest travel tips and trends.

Planning Your Itinerary with Virtual Tours

In the era of virtual travel, many museums, landmarks, and attractions in Pisa offer virtual tours and engaging experiences that enable you to explore from the convenience of your own home. Websites like Google Arts & Culture (https://artsandculture.google.com/) and Musei di Pisa (https://www.musei.pisa.it/) offer virtual exhibitions, 360-degree tours, and multimedia presentations that provide a glimpse into Pisa's rich cultural heritage.

By harnessing the power of useful websites, mobile apps, and online resources, you can plan, navigate, and enhance your visit to Pisa with confidence and ease. Whether you're seeking accommodation options, booking tours, or exploring virtual experiences, these online tools provide valuable assistance and insights to ensure a memorable and enjoyable travel experience in this enchanting Italian city.

5.8 Visitor Centers and Tourist Assistance

When visiting Pisa, it's comforting to know that there are dedicated visitor centers and tourist assistance services available to help make your experience as seamless and enjoyable as possible. One such resource is the Pisa Tourist Information Office, conveniently located near the iconic Leaning Tower in Piazza del Duomo. Here, friendly and knowledgeable staff members are ready to provide visitors with a wealth of information about the city's attractions, events, and services.

Utilizing Official Websites

Before your trip, consider exploring the official website of the Pisa Tourist Information Office (https://www.turismo.pisa.it/en/) to familiarize yourself with the services offered and access useful resources such as maps, guides, and event calendars. The website provides valuable information on accommodations, transportation options, dining recommendations, and upcoming cultural events, allowing you to plan your visit with ease.

Seeking Assistance at Airport and Train Stations

For travelers arriving by air or train, assistance is readily available at Pisa's airport and train stations. The Pisa International Airport (Galileo Galilei Airport) features an information desk staffed by multilingual personnel who can provide guidance on transportation options, airport facilities, and nearby attractions. Similarly, the Pisa Centrale railway station has a tourist information office where visitors can obtain maps, brochures, and assistance with travel-related inquiries.

Engaging with Local Guides and Tours

For those seeking personalized assistance and insights, guided tours led by knowledgeable local guides offer a fantastic way to explore Pisa's landmarks and hidden gems. Companies such as Walks of Italy (https://www.walksofitaly.com/) and City Wonders (https://www.citywonders.com/) offer a variety of guided tours, including walking tours of Pisa's historic center, guided visits to the Leaning Tower, and excursions to nearby attractions such as Lucca and Cinque Terre.

Connecting with Digital Resources

In addition to physical visitor centers and assistance services, digital resources such as mobile apps and online forums can be invaluable tools for accessing tourist information and assistance. Apps like TripAdvisor (https://www.tripadvisor.com/) and Yelp (https://www.yelp.com/) provide user-generated reviews, recommendations, and ratings for accommodations, restaurants, and attractions in Pisa, helping you make informed decisions during your stay.

Utilizing Emergency Contacts and Services

In the event of an emergency or if you require urgent assistance during your visit to Pisa, it's essential to know who to contact for help. The universal emergency number in Italy is 112, which connects you to police, ambulance, and fire services. Additionally, your country's embassy or consulate in Italy can provide support and assistance to citizens in need.

Visitor centers and tourist assistance services play a crucial role in ensuring a smooth and memorable travel experience in Pisa. Whether you need information on attractions, assistance with transportation, or guidance on local customs and etiquette, these resources are readily available to help you navigate the city with confidence and ease. By accessing official websites, engaging with local guides, and utilizing digital resources, you can make the most of your visit to this enchanting Italian destination.

CHAPTER 6
CULINARY DELIGHTS

6.1 Traditional Pisa Cuisine

Pisa, nestled in the heart of Tuscany, boasts a culinary tradition as rich and diverse as its storied history. From rustic peasant fare to refined delicacies, the city's traditional cuisine reflects the region's bountiful land and vibrant culture. Embark on a gastronomic journey through Pisa's traditional dishes, where each bite tells a story of centuries-old recipes and local flavors.

Cecina: A Taste of Tuscan Street Food

Begin your culinary adventure with a taste of "Cecina," a savory chickpea flour pancake that's a beloved staple of Tuscan street food. Found in local bakeries and street vendors throughout Pisa, Cecina is both affordable and satisfying, typically priced at around €2 to €3 per serving. Pair this crispy yet tender pancake with a drizzle of extra virgin olive oil and a sprinkle of black pepper for the perfect on-the-go snack.

Pappa al Pomodoro: A Rustic Tomato Delight

For a taste of comfort and nostalgia, indulge in a bowl of "Pappa al Pomodoro," a rustic tomato and bread soup that embodies the essence of Tuscan home cooking. Made with ripe tomatoes, garlic, basil, and stale bread soaked in vegetable broth, Pappa al Pomodoro offers a symphony of flavors that warm the soul. Prices for this hearty soup typically range from €6 to €10 per bowl, depending on the restaurant's ambiance and location.

Cacciucco: A Seafood Lover's Dream

Venture into the realm of seafood delights with "Cacciucco," a traditional Tuscan seafood stew brimming with the bounty of the Mediterranean Sea. Featuring a vibrant mix of fish and shellfish simmered in a rich tomato broth flavored with garlic, chili peppers, and aromatic herbs, Cacciucco is a culinary masterpiece that beckons seafood aficionados. Prices for this indulgent dish may vary depending on the selection of seafood and the restaurant's pricing, ranging from €15 to €30 per serving.

Pici: Hand-Rolled Pasta Perfection

No culinary journey through Pisa would be complete without sampling "Pici," a type of hand-rolled pasta that hails from the Tuscan region. Served with a variety of sauces, such as ragù (meat sauce), tomato and basil, or wild boar, Pici pasta offers a delightful texture and flavor that embodies the essence of Tuscan cuisine. Prices for Pici dishes typically range from €10 to €20, depending on the restaurant and accompanying sauce.

Navigating Prices and Dining Experiences

As you explore Pisa's culinary landscape, keep in mind that prices for traditional dishes may vary depending on the restaurant's location, ambiance, and reputation. Trattorias and osterias, which are traditional Italian eateries, often offer more affordable dining options compared to upscale restaurants. Budget-conscious travelers can expect to spend anywhere from €10 to €30 per person for a satisfying meal at a mid-range establishment.

Embark on a culinary journey through Pisa and discover the rich tapestry of flavors that define traditional Tuscan cuisine. From the humble Cecina to the luxurious Cacciucco, each dish tells a story of Pisa's culinary heritage and offers a glimpse into the region's vibrant culture. Whether you're indulging in street food delights or savoring a leisurely meal at a local trattoria, immerse yourself in the flavors of Pisa and create unforgettable memories of your gastronomic adventure in this charming Italian city.

6.2 Local Delicacies and Street Food

In the bustling streets of Pisa, amidst the centuries-old architecture and vibrant piazzas, lies a hidden gem of culinary delights: the city's eclectic street food scene. From savory snacks to sweet treats, Pisa's local delicacies and street food offerings are a testament to the region's rich culinary heritage and diverse flavors.

Panini Toscani: A Sandwich with Tuscan Flair

For a quick and delicious meal on the streets of Pisa, indulge in a "Panino Toscano," a classic Tuscan sandwich bursting with flavor. Made with crusty bread, slices of flavorful Tuscan salami, pecorino cheese, and a drizzle of extra virgin olive oil, Panini Toscani are a savory delight that embodies the region's culinary traditions. Prices for these hearty sandwiches vary depending on the ingredients and the vendor, typically ranging from €5 to €8 per sandwich.

Schiacciata: A Tuscan Twist on Flatbread

Another popular street food in Pisa is "Schiacciata," a rustic Tuscan flatbread that's perfect for satisfying your cravings on the go. Similar to focaccia, Schiacciata is topped with a variety of savory ingredients such as tomatoes, olives, herbs, and cheese, creating a mouthwatering combination of flavors and textures. Prices for Schiacciata vary depending on the toppings and the size of the portion, with prices typically ranging from €3 to €5 per piece.

Gelato: Sweet Treats on Every Corner

No visit to Pisa would be complete without indulging in a scoop or two of authentic Italian gelato. With gelaterias dotting the city streets, you'll have no trouble finding this creamy and refreshing treat in a variety of flavors. Prices for gelato vary depending on the size of the serving and the number of scoops, with prices typically ranging from €2 to €5 per cone or cup.

Navigating Prices and Locations

As you explore Pisa's street food scene, keep in mind that prices may vary depending on the vendor, location, and quality of ingredients. Budget-conscious travelers can find affordable options at local markets, bakeries, and street food stalls, while those seeking a more upscale experience can opt for gourmet food trucks or specialty shops.

From the savory delights of Cecina to the sweet indulgence of gelato, Pisa's local delicacies and street food offerings are sure to delight your senses and satisfy your cravings. So, take a stroll through the charming streets of Pisa, follow your nose to the tantalizing aromas wafting from food carts and bakeries, and embark on a culinary adventure that will leave you with a taste of Tuscan tradition and memories to cherish for a lifetime.

6.3 Dining Experiences: Restaurants and Trattorias

Pisa isn't just about its iconic landmarks like the Leaning Tower; it's also a city that boasts a dynamic culinary landscape, providing a variety of upscale dining venues that cater to sophisticated tastes Prepare to embark on a gastronomic journey through Pisa's gourmet experiences, where exquisite flavors and impeccable service converge to create unforgettable dining memories.

Ristorante Grotta di Leo

Nestled in the heart of Pisa's historic center, Ristorante Grotta di Leo stands out as a beacon of culinary excellence. Located just a stone's throw away from the Leaning Tower, this Michelin-starred restaurant offers a sophisticated dining experience characterized by creative interpretations of traditional Tuscan cuisine. Guests can expect meticulously crafted dishes showcasing locally sourced ingredients, paired with an extensive wine list featuring prestigious labels from Italy's renowned vineyards.

La Mescita

For a gourmet experience with a modern twist, head to La Mescita, a stylish restaurant housed within a beautifully restored 15th-century building. Situated near Piazza dei Cavalieri, this culinary gem seamlessly blends traditional Tuscan flavors with innovative techniques, resulting in a menu that surprises and delights the senses. From delicate seafood dishes to succulent meat entrees, La Mescita offers a tantalizing culinary journey that showcases the best of both local and international cuisine.

Ristorante Galileo

Located on the banks of the Arno River, Ristorante Galileo has been a fixture in Pisa's dining scene for over a century, earning a reputation for its impeccable service and refined culinary offerings. The restaurant's elegant dining room exudes old-world charm, providing the perfect backdrop for indulging in a gourmet feast. Guests can choose from an array of expertly prepared dishes, including fresh seafood, tender meats, and decadent desserts, all served with a touch of Tuscan hospitality.

Il Toscano

For those seeking an authentic taste of Tuscany, look no further than Il Toscano, a cozy trattoria located in the heart of Pisa's historic district. This charming restaurant prides itself on showcasing the region's culinary heritage through a menu of traditional Tuscan dishes prepared with passion and expertise. From hearty ribollita soup to tender bistecca alla fiorentina, every dish at Il Toscano is a celebration of local flavors and seasonal ingredients.

Navigating Prices and Reservations

As with any fine dining experience, prices at Pisa's gourmet restaurants can vary depending on factors such as location, reputation, and menu offerings. While some establishments may offer prix fixe menus or tasting menus, others may have à la carte options with prices ranging from €30 to €100 or more per person, excluding beverages. Additionally, it's advisable to make reservations in advance, especially during peak tourist seasons, to secure a table at your desired restaurant.

From Michelin-starred establishments to cozy trattorias, Pisa offers a diverse array of fine dining experiences that cater to every taste and preference. Whether you're indulging in innovative fusion cuisine or savoring classic Tuscan flavors, dining in Pisa is an unforgettable journey that promises to delight your senses and leave you with lasting culinary memories. So, don your finest attire, prepare your palate for a feast, and embark on a gastronomic odyssey through the flavors of Pisa.

6.4 Wine Tasting and Vineyard Tours

Pisa, nestled in the heart of the Tuscan countryside, offers visitors a unique opportunity to immerse themselves in the rich tradition of winemaking that has flourished in the region for centuries. Wine tasting and vineyard tours provide an intimate glimpse into the artistry and craftsmanship behind some of Italy's most renowned wines, allowing visitors to savor the flavors of Tuscany while exploring its picturesque landscapes.

Discovering Charming Vineyards

Embark on a journey through Pisa's vineyards, where rolling hills dotted with vineyards and olive groves create a breathtaking backdrop for wine tasting adventures. Many vineyards in the Pisa area welcome visitors for guided tours and tastings, offering insights into the winemaking process and the opportunity to sample a diverse selection of wines, from crisp whites to full-bodied reds.

Visiting Family-Owned Estates

One of the highlights of wine tasting in Pisa is the chance to visit family-owned estates that have been producing wine for generations. These intimate settings provide a more personal and authentic experience, allowing visitors to connect with winemakers and learn about their time-honored traditions and techniques. Whether you're strolling through vineyards, touring historic cellars, or enjoying a leisurely tasting overlooking the countryside, each visit offers a glimpse into the passion and dedication that goes into every bottle of Tuscan wine.

Sampling Tuscan Varietals
During wine tastings, visitors can expect to sample a variety of Tuscan wines, including Sangiovese, the region's flagship grape variety, known for its vibrant acidity and cherry-forward flavors. Other varietals commonly found in Pisa include Vernaccia di San Gimignano, a crisp white wine with floral and citrus notes, and Supertuscans, innovative blends that combine traditional Tuscan grapes with international varieties. Tastings often include a selection of reds, whites, and sometimes rosés, allowing visitors to explore the diverse terroir and winemaking styles of the region.

Understanding Terroir and Wine Pairing
As you sample different wines, knowledgeable guides will often provide insights into the terroir, or the unique combination of soil, climate, and geography that shapes each wine's character. They may also offer suggestions for food pairings, showcasing the versatility of Tuscan wines when enjoyed alongside local cuisine. From aged Pecorino cheese to hearty Tuscan stews, there's no shortage of delicious pairings to complement the region's wines.

Considering Tour Fees and Reservations
While some vineyard tours and tastings may be complimentary or included with the purchase of wine, others may require advance reservations and incur a fee. Prices for vineyard tours and tastings can vary depending on the winery, the number of wines sampled, and any additional amenities or experiences offered. It's advisable to research and book tours in advance, especially during peak tourist seasons, to ensure availability and secure your spot.

Wine tasting and vineyard tours in Pisa offer a captivating blend of history, culture, and gastronomy, inviting visitors to savor the essence of Tuscany one sip at a time. Whether you're exploring centuries-old estates or sampling innovative blends at modern wineries, each experience promises to deepen your appreciation for Tuscan wine and leave you with lasting memories of your time in this enchanting region. So, raise a glass to Tuscan hospitality and embark on a journey through Pisa's vineyards, where every tasting is a celebration of the art of winemaking.

6.5 Cooking Classes and Culinary Workshops

Pisa isn't just a city of architectural wonders like the Leaning Tower; it's also a hub for culinary enthusiasts eager to delve into the secrets of Tuscan cuisine. Cooking classes and culinary workshops offer visitors a unique opportunity to roll up their sleeves, don an apron, and immerse themselves in the art of Italian cooking. Let's explore some of the top options for culinary experiences in Pisa.

Tuscan Cooking School

Located in the heart of Pisa's historic center, the Tuscan Cooking School invites participants to discover the essence of Tuscan gastronomy through immersive cooking classes led by expert chefs. Here, visitors can learn to prepare traditional Tuscan dishes such as handmade pasta, hearty soups, and succulent meat dishes using fresh, locally sourced ingredients. Classes typically range from €60 to €100 per person and include hands-on instruction, recipe demonstrations, and a delicious meal paired with local wines.

Culinary Workshops at La Scuola di Cucina

La Scuola di Cucina offers a range of culinary workshops and cooking classes designed to introduce participants to the rich flavors and techniques of Italian cuisine. From pizza-making workshops to pasta masterclasses, visitors can choose from a variety of hands-on experiences tailored to their interests and skill levels. Led by passionate chefs with a deep appreciation for local ingredients, these workshops provide a fun and educational way to explore the culinary heritage of Pisa and Tuscany. Prices for workshops vary depending on the duration and type of class, with rates starting from €50 per person.

Olive Oil Tasting and Cooking Experience at Fattoria di Poggiopiano

For a truly immersive culinary experience, consider joining an olive oil tasting and cooking workshop at Fattoria di Poggiopiano, a charming agriturismo nestled in the picturesque Tuscan countryside. Participants will have the opportunity to taste a selection of extra virgin olive oils produced on the estate, learn about the olive oil production process, and discover how to incorporate this liquid gold into their cooking. Following the tasting, guests can roll up their sleeves and join a hands-on cooking class led by local chefs, where they'll learn to prepare traditional Tuscan dishes using olive oil as a key ingredient. Prices for the olive oil tasting and cooking experience start from €80 per person and include all materials, ingredients, and a delicious meal paired with local wines.

Booking and Additional Information

Advance reservations are highly recommended for cooking classes and culinary workshops in Pisa, especially during peak tourist seasons. Participants should wear comfortable clothing and closed-toe shoes suitable for cooking activities. Most cooking classes and workshops cater to both beginners and experienced cooks, so don't hesitate to join in regardless of your skill level. Whether you're looking to master the art of pasta-making or simply indulge in a fun and educational culinary experience, cooking classes and workshops in Pisa offer a memorable way to explore the flavors of Tuscany and create lasting memories of your visit to this enchanting Italian city.

CHAPTER 7
CULTURE AND HERITAGE

7.1 Historical Landmarks and Monuments

Nestled along the banks of the Arno River in the picturesque region of Tuscany, Pisa beckons visitors with its rich tapestry of history and timeless beauty. As you wander through its cobbled streets and sun-drenched piazzas, you'll encounter a variety of historical landmarks and monuments that attest to the city's remarkable past.. From iconic architectural wonders to hidden gems tucked away in quiet corners, each site tells a story of Pisa's enduring legacy and cultural heritage.

The Leaning Tower of Pisa

No visit to Pisa is complete without marveling at the iconic Leaning Tower, one of the most recognized landmarks in the world. Standing proudly in Piazza dei Miracoli (Square of Miracles), this medieval bell tower captivates visitors with its distinctive tilt, a result of centuries of engineering marvels and architectural mysteries. Ascend the tower's spiraling staircase to enjoy panoramic views of Pisa's skyline and the surrounding countryside, and be sure to capture the perfect photo angle to immortalize your visit.

Piazza dei Miracoli

Surrounding the Leaning Tower, Piazza dei Miracoli serves as the beating heart of Pisa's cultural heritage. This UNESCO World Heritage Site encompasses a breathtaking ensemble of architectural masterpieces, including the iconic Duomo (Cathedral), Baptistery, and Camposanto (Monumental Cemetery). Take a leisurely stroll through the square's manicured lawns and marble facades, and soak in the serene ambiance while marveling at the intricate details of these historic monuments.

Pisa Cathedral (Duomo)

Step inside the magnificent Pisa Cathedral, a stunning masterpiece of Romanesque architecture that showcases the city's religious and artistic legacy. Admire the intricately carved façade adorned with marble columns, mosaics, and sculptures, and venture inside to explore its cavernous interior adorned with priceless artworks, intricate frescoes, and ornate stained glass windows. Don't miss the chance to admire the pulpit sculpted by Giovanni Pisano and the majestic bronze doors crafted by Bonanno Pisano, which stand as testaments to the city's artistic prowess.

Baptistery of St. John
Adjacent to the cathedral stands the Baptistery of St. John, a sublime example of Pisan Romanesque architecture. Marvel at the Baptistery's elegant marble exterior, crowned by a majestic dome and adorned with intricate sculptures and reliefs depicting biblical scenes and saints. Venture inside to admire the acoustics of the octagonal interior, and gaze up at the breathtaking ceiling adorned with intricate paintings and golden mosaics that tell stories of salvation and redemption.

Camposanto Monumentale
Complete your exploration of Piazza dei Miracoli with a visit to the Camposanto Monumentale, or Monumental Cemetery, a sacred resting place that holds the remains of Pisa's noble families and prominent citizens. Wander through its serene cloisters adorned with ancient tombs, sarcophagi, and funerary monuments, and contemplate the passage of time amidst the tranquil beauty of its marble arcades and lush gardens.

As you bid farewell to Pisa's historical landmarks and monuments, you'll carry with you not only memories of its architectural wonders but also a deeper appreciation for the city's rich history and cultural heritage. From the leaning tower that defies gravity to the sacred sanctuaries that echo with centuries of devotion, each site offers a glimpse into Pisa's past and an invitation to embark on a journey of discovery through the annals of time. So, pack your curiosity and wanderlust, and let Pisa's historical treasures captivate your imagination and inspire your soul.

7.2 Art and Architecture

Welcome to Pisa, a city where art and architecture intertwine to create a captivating tapestry of beauty and creativity. As you wander through its winding streets and historic squares, you'll encounter an array of artistic treasures that reflect the city's rich cultural heritage and enduring legacy. From majestic cathedrals adorned with intricate sculptures to charming Renaissance palaces adorned with frescoes, Pisa's artistic landscape offers a feast for the senses and a glimpse into the soul of the city.

Romanesque Marvels

Pisa's architectural heritage is deeply rooted in the Romanesque style, characterized by its robust stone structures, rounded arches, and decorative motifs. One of the finest examples of Romanesque architecture in Pisa is the Cathedral of Santa Maria Assunta, a magnificent masterpiece that dominates the city's skyline with its imposing façade and elegant bell tower. Marvel at the cathedral's intricately carved reliefs, majestic bronze doors, and soaring columns, and admire the craftsmanship of its master builders and artisans.

Gothic Grandeur

As the medieval period gave way to the Gothic era, Pisa witnessed the rise of new architectural styles characterized by soaring spires, pointed arches, and intricate detailing. The Baptistery of St. John stands as a prime example of Gothic architecture in Pisa, with its graceful marble exterior and towering dome that reaches towards the heavens. Step inside to marvel at the play of light and shadow cast by the stained glass windows, and admire the delicate tracery of the vaulted ceilings that evoke a sense of divine transcendence.

Renaissance Splendor

During the Renaissance, Pisa experienced a cultural renaissance of its own, as artists and architects sought to revive the classical ideals of beauty, proportion, and harmony. The Piazza dei Cavalieri emerged as a hub of Renaissance architecture and art, with its elegant palaces and statues celebrating the glory of the Medici dynasty. Visit the

Palazzo della Carovana, adorned with frescoes by Giorgio Vasari, and marvel at the grandeur of the Knights' Square, where history comes alive amidst the timeless beauty of its architectural masterpieces.

Artistic Treasures

In addition to its architectural wonders, Pisa is home to a wealth of artistic treasures housed in its museums, galleries, and churches. Discover masterpieces by renowned artists such as Andrea Pisano, Nicola Pisano, and Simone Martini at the Museo dell'Opera del Duomo, and admire the intricate detailing of medieval sculptures and reliefs that adorn the city's churches and civic buildings. Don't miss the chance to explore the vibrant contemporary art scene in Pisa, with its eclectic galleries and avant-garde exhibitions that push the boundaries of artistic expression.

As you immerse yourself in Pisa's arts and architecture, you'll find yourself transported through time and space, from the grandeur of the Romanesque cathedrals to the elegance of Renaissance palaces. Each artistic masterpiece tells a story of creativity, craftsmanship, and cultural heritage, inviting you to embark on a journey of discovery through the heart of Pisa. So, come explore the city's artistic soul, and let its beauty and brilliance inspire your own creative spirit.

7.3 Religious Sites and Traditions

Pisa is not only renowned for its iconic Leaning Tower but also for its rich spiritual heritage. Steeped in centuries of religious tradition, the city is home to a myriad of sacred sites that bear witness to its profound spiritual significance. As you embark on a journey through Pisa's religious landscape, prepare to immerse yourself in a world of timeless traditions, awe-inspiring architecture, and profound spirituality.

Pisa Cathedral (Duomo di Pisa)

At the center of Pisa's spiritual center lies the magnificent Pisa Cathedral, a stunning masterpiece of Romanesque architecture dedicated to Santa Maria Assunta (Saint Mary of the Assumption). As you approach the cathedral, you'll be captivated by its intricate façade adorned with marble columns, sculptures, and exquisite mosaics. Step inside to behold the cathedral's cavernous interior, where the soft glow of stained glass windows illuminates the sacred space, and marvel at the ornate pulpit sculpted by Giovanni Pisano. Don't miss the opportunity to climb the cathedral's majestic dome for panoramic views of Pisa and beyond.

Baptistery of St. John (Battistero di San Giovanni)
Adjacent to the cathedral stands the Baptistery of St. John, a sublime testament to Pisa's enduring faith and architectural prowess. This magnificent structure, renowned for its acoustics and harmonious design, is dedicated to St. John the Baptist and serves as a sacred space for baptismal rituals and ceremonies. Admire the Baptistery's elegant marble exterior and intricate reliefs depicting biblical scenes, then step inside to experience the serenity of its octagonal interior, where echoes of centuries-old prayers still linger.

San Piero a Grado: A Sanctuary of Serenity
For a tranquil escape from the hustle and bustle of the city center, venture to San Piero a Grado, a charming church nestled amidst lush greenery just outside of Pisa. This ancient sanctuary, believed to have been founded in the 4th century, is steeped in legend and lore, with ties to the Apostle Peter and early Christian missionaries. Wander through its peaceful grounds and contemplate the sacredness of the site, where pilgrims have sought solace and spiritual renewal for centuries.

Religious Traditions and Festivals
Throughout the year, Pisa comes alive with a vibrant tapestry of religious traditions and festivals that celebrate the city's deep-rooted faith and cultural heritage. From solemn processions during Holy Week to joyous celebrations honoring patron saints, visitors have the opportunity to witness age-old rituals and participate in sacred ceremonies that have been passed down through generations. Don't miss the chance to experience the enchanting spectacle of the Luminara di San Ranieri, a magical evening procession

illuminated by thousands of flickering candles that light up the city's historic streets and waterways.

As you explore Pisa's religious sites and traditions, you'll discover more than just architectural wonders and sacred spaces; you'll encounter a profound sense of connection to the spiritual essence of the city and its people. Whether you're admiring the grandeur of the cathedral, meditating in the tranquil surroundings of a centuries-old church, or participating in a time-honored festival, Pisa offers a journey of spiritual discovery that transcends time and space. So, open your heart to the whispers of ancient prayers and the echoes of centuries-old traditions, and let the spiritual essence of Pisa enrich your soul and inspire your journey of faith.

7.4 Cultural Events and Festivals

All through the year, the city buzzes with numerous events and festivals honoring its rich heritage, artistic talent, and community spirit. From vibrant processions to energetic music showcases, each cultural event provides visitors with a special chance to delve into the essence of Pisa's traditions and celebrations.

Gioco del Ponte

One of Pisa's most iconic cultural events is the Gioco del Ponte, or Battle of the Bridge, which takes place annually on the last Sunday of June. Dating back to the 16th century, this historical reenactment commemorates the city's medieval past and the strategic importance of its bridges. Participants don traditional costumes representing the city's rival districts and engage in a spirited tug-of-war competition atop the Ponte di Mezzo bridge. The event culminates in a spectacular fireworks display over the Arno River, creating a captivating spectacle that draws crowds from near and far.

Luminara di San Ranieri

Every year on the evening of June 16th, Pisa's historic center is illuminated by the soft glow of thousands of candles during the Luminara di San Ranieri. This enchanting festival pays homage to the city's patron saint, San Ranieri, and marks the eve of his feast day. Visitors can wander through the streets lined with flickering candles, admiring the illuminated facades of buildings and monuments, including the iconic Leaning Tower. The atmosphere is imbued with a sense of reverence and magic, as locals and visitors alike come together to celebrate this centuries-old tradition.

Pisa Book Festival

For book lovers and literary enthusiasts, the Pisa Book Festival held in October is a must-attend event. This annual celebration of literature brings together authors, publishers, and book enthusiasts from across Italy and beyond. Visitors can browse through a diverse array of book stalls, attend author talks and panel discussions, and participate in writing workshops and literary events. Whether you're an avid book lover or just intrigued by the world of literature, the Pisa Book Festival provides a vibrant and inspiring environment that celebrates the written word in all its diversity.

Pisa Jazz Festival

Music aficionados flock to Pisa each year for the Pisa Jazz Festival, a week-long extravaganza held in November that showcases the best of contemporary jazz music. From intimate club performances to open-air concerts in historic piazzas, the festival offers a diverse lineup of world-renowned jazz artists and emerging talents. Visitors can immerse themselves in the soulful rhythms and improvisational melodies of jazz while soaking up the vibrant atmosphere of Pisa's music scene. Whether you're a seasoned jazz enthusiast or simply looking to discover new sounds, the Pisa Jazz Festival promises a memorable musical experience.

As you explore the cultural events and festivals of Pisa, you'll discover a city that pulsates with creativity, tradition, and a deep sense of community. Whether you're marveling at the spectacle of the Gioco del Ponte, basking in the glow of the Luminara di San Ranieri, delving into the world of literature at the Pisa Book Festival, or tapping your toes to the rhythms of jazz at the Pisa Jazz Festival, each event offers a unique window into the city's cultural soul. So, pack your curiosity and join in the festivities, as you embark on a journey to uncover the vibrant cultural tapestry of Pisa.

7.5 Preservation Efforts and Heritage Conservation

Pisa, with its rich tapestry of historical landmarks and cultural heritage, stands as a testament to the enduring legacy of human creativity and ingenuity. As visitors traverse the streets of this ancient city, they are greeted by magnificent monuments, centuries-old buildings, and treasured artifacts that serve as guardians of Pisa's past. Behind the scenes, however, dedicated efforts are underway to preserve and protect these invaluable treasures for future generations to cherish and appreciate.

Historical Significance and Challenges

Pisa's cultural heritage is not only a source of pride for its inhabitants but also a magnet for tourists from around the globe. The city's historical significance, however, also poses unique challenges in terms of conservation and preservation. With structures dating back centuries, such as the iconic Leaning Tower and the majestic Pisa Cathedral, ensuring their longevity requires meticulous care and attention to detail.

Conservation Practices and Techniques

To safeguard Pisa's architectural treasures, conservationists employ a variety of practices and techniques aimed at preventing deterioration and maintaining the structural integrity of these iconic landmarks. This includes regular inspections, monitoring of environmental factors, and implementation of restoration projects using traditional materials and craftsmanship techniques. Additionally, innovative technologies, such as laser scanning and 3D modeling, are employed to document and analyze the condition of historic structures with unprecedented precision.

Collaborative Partnerships

Preservation efforts in Pisa are often the result of collaborative partnerships between government agencies, conservation organizations, academic institutions, and local communities. These partnerships facilitate the sharing of knowledge, resources, and expertise, ensuring a holistic approach to heritage conservation. Furthermore, engagement with stakeholders, including residents and visitors alike, fosters a sense of ownership and responsibility towards preserving Pisa's cultural legacy.

Community Involvement and Education

Empowering local communities to take an active role in heritage conservation is paramount to the long-term sustainability of preservation efforts. Educational initiatives, workshops, and public outreach programs are organized to raise awareness about the importance of cultural heritage and the role individuals can play in its protection. By instilling a sense of pride and appreciation for their heritage, communities become stewards of Pisa's cultural treasures, actively contributing to their preservation.

Challenges and Future Outlook

Despite the concerted efforts to preserve Pisa's cultural heritage, challenges such as urban development pressures, environmental factors, and budget constraints continue to pose significant obstacles. As the city evolves and modernizes, finding a delicate balance between progress and preservation remains a constant challenge. Looking ahead, it is imperative to adopt sustainable conservation strategies that respect Pisa's past while embracing the opportunities of the future.

In the face of evolving landscapes and changing times, the commitment to preserving Pisa's cultural heritage remains unwavering. Through collaborative efforts, innovative approaches, and community engagement, conservationists, and stakeholders alike continue to protect the city's architectural gems, ensuring that Pisa's abundant heritage lasts for generations to come. As visitors marvel at the splendor of Pisa's historic landmarks, they can take comfort in knowing that behind each façade lies a dedicated effort to preserve the stories of the past for the enjoyment of future travelers.

CHAPTER 8

OUTDOOR ACTIVITIES AND ADVENTURES

8.1 Walking Tours and Sightseeing

Embarking on a walking tour of Pisa offers visitors a captivating journey through centuries of history, culture, and architectural splendor. As you traverse the city's charming streets and piazzas, you'll encounter iconic landmarks, hidden gems, and vibrant neighborhoods that paint a vivid picture of Pisa's rich heritage. Let's embark on a virtual stroll through Pisa's most enchanting sights and discover the beauty that awaits around every corner.

Strolling Along the Arno River
Follow the gentle flow of the Arno River as you meander along its picturesque banks, offering panoramic views of Pisa's skyline and the surrounding countryside. Admire the elegant bridges that span the river, such as Ponte di Mezzo and Ponte Solferino, and watch as locals and visitors alike gather along the riverbanks to enjoy leisurely strolls, picnics, and boat rides.

Exploring Historic Neighborhoods

Venture beyond the tourist hotspots and explore Pisa's historic neighborhoods, each with its own unique charm and character. Wander through the narrow alleyways of the San Martino district, lined with quaint cafes, artisan shops, and centuries-old buildings. Discover the vibrant atmosphere of the Borgo Stretto, a bustling thoroughfare filled with boutiques, gelaterias, and lively street performers. As you wander, keep an eye out for hidden courtyards, ancient churches, and colorful street art that add to the city's allure.

Admiring Architectural Marvels

Pisa's streets are adorned with a wealth of architectural treasures waiting to be discovered. Marvel at the grandeur of Palazzo dei Cavalieri, a stunning Renaissance palace adorned with intricate façades and elegant courtyards. Pause to admire the medieval towers that punctuate the city's skyline, such as Torre dei Gualandi and Torre della Muda, each with its own fascinating history and legends.

Culinary Delights and Local Flavors

No walking tour of Pisa would be complete without sampling the city's culinary delights. Take a break from sightseeing to indulge in a gelato from one of Pisa's beloved gelaterias, savor a slice of traditional Tuscan pizza, or sip on a refreshing glass of Chianti at a cozy enoteca. As you dine alfresco on Pisa's charming piazzas, you'll experience the true essence of Italian hospitality and gastronomy.

As you conclude your walking tour of Pisa, you'll carry with you memories of enchanting sights, delightful flavors, and warm hospitality that will linger long after you've bid farewell to this captivating city. Whether you're admiring architectural marvels, strolling along the riverbanks, or savoring local delicacies, each step reveals a new layer of Pisa's timeless charm and invites you to immerse yourself in its rich tapestry of history and culture. So embrace the adventurous spirit, and set off on a journey through the streets of Pisa that guarantees to enchant the senses and leave a lasting imprint on your heart.

8.2 Cycling Routes and Bike Tours

As visitors explore the enchanting city of Pisa, there's no better way to soak in its charm and beauty than by embarking on a cycling adventure. With its flat terrain, picturesque landscapes, and network of cycling routes, Pisa offers cyclists of all levels the perfect opportunity to discover its hidden gems and iconic landmarks on two wheels. Whether you're a leisure cyclist seeking a scenic ride or a seasoned enthusiast craving an adrenaline-pumping tour, Pisa has something for everyone.

Cycling Routes: Exploring the City and Beyond

Pisa boasts a variety of cycling routes that cater to different interests and preferences. From leisurely rides along the Arno River to challenging routes through the Tuscan countryside, cyclists can choose from a range of options to suit their desired pace and distance. The city's well-maintained bike paths and designated cycling lanes make it safe and convenient to explore both urban areas and rural landscapes.

Arno River Cycling Path: Riverside Serenity

One of the most popular cycling routes in Pisa is along the scenic Arno River. This flat and leisurely path meanders alongside the tranquil waters of the river, offering cyclists stunning views of the city's historic buildings, charming bridges, and lush greenery. Whether you're out for a morning workout or a leisurely afternoon ride, pausing along the way to take in the sights, snap photos, and soak up the vibrant atmosphere of the city's bustling streets.

Lucca-Pisa Cycle Path

For those seeking a longer and more immersive cycling experience, the Lucca-Pisa cycle path offers a scenic journey through the picturesque Tuscan countryside. Starting in the historic city of Lucca, this well-marked route winds its way through vineyards, olive groves, and medieval villages, offering cyclists the chance to explore the region's rich history and breathtaking landscapes. With options for guided tours or self-guided rides, cyclists can customize their journey to suit their interests and abilities.

Pisa City Center

Exploring Pisa's city center by bike allows visitors to cover more ground while immersing themselves in the city's rich history and cultural heritage. Cyclists can pedal past iconic landmarks such as the Leaning Tower, Piazza dei Miracoli, and Pisa Cathedral, pausing along the way to take in the sights, snap photos, and soak up the vibrant atmosphere of the city's bustling streets. With plenty of bike-friendly cafés and restaurants dotted throughout the city, cyclists can refuel with delicious Tuscan cuisine after a day of sightseeing.

Bike Tours

For those looking for a more immersive and informative experience, guided bike tours offer the perfect blend of adventure and education. Knowledgeable local guides lead cyclists on curated routes, providing insights into Pisa's history, culture, and culinary traditions along the way. Whether it's a themed tour focusing on art and architecture or a gastronomic journey through the city's culinary delights, bike tours offer a unique perspective and a deeper appreciation for Pisa's treasures.

Practical Considerations

Renting bikes in Pisa is easy, with numerous rental shops and bike-sharing programs available throughout the city. Cyclists should ensure they have appropriate safety gear, including helmets and reflective clothing, and familiarize themselves with local traffic laws and cycling etiquette. It's also advisable to carry a map or GPS device to navigate the city's streets and trails effectively.

Whether you're exploring the city's historic landmarks, pedaling through picturesque landscapes, or joining a guided bike tour, cycling in Pisa offers a unique and memorable way to experience this captivating city. So, hop on a bike, feel the wind in your hair, and let the adventure begin as you discover the beauty and charm of Pisa from a whole new perspective.

8.3 River Cruises and Boat Tours

Embarking on a river cruise or boat tour in Pisa offers a delightful way to experience the city's charm and beauty from a unique perspective. As you glide along the tranquil waters of the Arno River, you'll be treated to stunning views of Pisa's iconic landmarks and picturesque landscapes. Let's delve into the details of these enchanting river cruises and boat tours, including costs, schedules, and what to expect.

River Cruises Along the Arno

One of the most popular ways to explore Pisa by river is through a guided river cruise along the Arno. These cruises typically last around one to two hours and offer narrated Tours available in multiple languages offer intriguing insights into the city's history and architecture. Prices for river cruises vary depending on the duration and amenities included, with most tours ranging from €15 to €30 per person. Some companies may offer discounts for children or group bookings.

Sunset Boat Tours

For those seeking a romantic experience, sunset boat tours along the Arno River offer a magical setting to watch the sun dip below the horizon while basking in the glow of twilight. These tours often include a glass of prosecco or local wine to toast to the beauty of the moment. Prices for sunset boat tours typically range from €25 to €50 per person, depending on the duration and inclusions. Advance reservations are recommended, especially during peak tourist seasons.

Boat Tours to the Tuscan Countryside

For a more immersive experience, consider booking a boat tour that ventures beyond the city limits to explore the scenic Tuscan countryside surrounding Pisa. These tours may include visits to nearby villages, vineyards, and olive groves, allowing participants to sample local delicacies and wines along the way. Prices for countryside boat tours vary depending on the itinerary and activities included, with full-day excursions typically ranging from €50 to €100 per person.

Practical Information and Tips

Before embarking on a river cruise or boat tour in Pisa, it's essential to consider a few practicalities. Be sure to check the departure times and meeting points for your chosen tour, as well as any specific instructions provided by the tour operator. Dress comfortably and bring sunscreen, a hat, and sunglasses to protect yourself from the sun's rays, especially during the warmer months. Additionally, don't forget to charge your camera or smartphone to capture the breathtaking views along the way.

Whether you opt for a leisurely river cruise along the Arno, a romantic sunset boat tour, or an adventure to the Tuscan countryside, exploring Pisa by river promises unforgettable experiences and breathtaking vistas. With options to suit every budget and preference, these boat tours offer a captivating glimpse into the city's rich history, culture, and natural beauty. So, set sail on a journey of discovery, and let Pisa's waterways enchant you with their timeless allure.

8.4 Hiking Trails and Nature Reserves

Beyond its historic landmarks and architectural wonders, Pisa offers visitors the opportunity to immerse themselves in the serene beauty of its natural landscapes. From lush forests to tranquil nature reserves, the city boasts an array of hiking trails and outdoor destinations waiting to be explored. Let's embark on a journey through Pisa's hiking trails and nature reserves, discovering the beauty of its wilderness and the wonders of its flora and fauna.

Hiking Trails Amidst Tuscan Landscapes

Pisa is blessed with an abundance of hiking trails that wind their way through picturesque countryside, offering stunning views of rolling hills, vineyards, and olive groves. One popular trail is the Monti Pisani Circuit, which encompasses a network of paths that traverse the scenic hillsides of the Monti Pisani mountain range. Hikers can choose from various routes of varying lengths and difficulty levels, making it suitable for both beginners and experienced trekkers alike.

Exploring Nature Reserves

For those seeking a more immersive nature experience, Pisa is home to several nature reserves that protect and preserve its diverse ecosystems. The Migliarino, San Rossore, and Massaciuccoli Regional Park, located just a short distance from the city center, offers visitors the chance to explore pristine marshlands, pine forests, and sandy beaches. Guided nature walks and birdwatching tours are available, providing insight into the region's rich biodiversity and wildlife habitats.

The Charm of Coastal Trails

Pisa's proximity to the coast provides hikers with the opportunity to explore scenic coastal trails that offer panoramic views of the Ligurian Sea. The Path of Love (Sentiero dell'Amore), which stretches along the rugged coastline of the Cinque Terre region, is a popular choice for those seeking breathtaking vistas and picturesque seaside villages. While not located directly in Pisa, the Cinque Terre can be reached within a few hours by train, making it an ideal day trip destination for outdoor enthusiasts.

Practical Information and Tips

Before embarking on a hiking adventure in Pisa, it's essential to consider a few practicalities. Check the weather forecast and trail conditions beforehand, and dress appropriately for the terrain and climate. Wear sturdy hiking shoes, bring plenty of water, and pack snacks and sunscreen for the journey. Additionally, be mindful of any wildlife encounters and follow Leave No Trace principles to minimize your impact on the environment.

As you traverse the hiking trails and nature reserves of Pisa, you'll discover a world of natural beauty and tranquility waiting to be explored. Whether you're marveling at panoramic vistas from the Monti Pisani, spotting migratory birds in the regional park, or strolling along coastal paths overlooking the sea, each experience offers a glimpse into the unspoiled wilderness of Tuscany. So, lace up your hiking boots, breathe in the fresh air, and embark on a journey of discovery through Pisa's natural treasures.

8.5 Adventure Sports: Climbing, Rafting, etc.

While Pisa is renowned for its cultural heritage and historical landmarks, it also offers adrenaline-seekers the opportunity to partake in a variety of exhilarating adventure sports. From rock climbing to white-water rafting, the city and its surrounding areas boast a plethora of outdoor activities that promise heart-pounding excitement and unforgettable thrills. Let's delve into the world of adventure sports in Pisa, exploring the adrenaline-fueled experiences awaiting intrepid travelers.

Rock Climbing in the Tuscan Countryside

For avid climbers and outdoor enthusiasts, Pisa's rugged landscapes provide an ideal playground for rock climbing adventures. The Monte Pisano mountain range, located just a short distance from the city center, offers numerous climbing routes suitable for climbers of all skill levels. From limestone cliffs to granite crags, these natural formations provide thrilling challenges and breathtaking views of the surrounding countryside. While many climbing areas are accessible for free, guided climbing tours and equipment rental may be available for a fee, ranging from €30 to €100 per person depending on the duration and services included.

White-Water Rafting on the Serchio River

For those craving a splash of adrenaline, white-water rafting on the Serchio River offers an exhilarating experience amidst Pisa's natural beauty. Guided rafting tours take participants on thrilling journeys through rapids and cascading waters, providing an adrenaline rush like no other. Tours typically last half a day to a full day, with prices ranging from €50 to €100 per person, inclusive of equipment rental and professional guides. Whether you're a seasoned rafter or a first-time adventurer, white-water rafting in Pisa promises an unforgettable aquatic adventure.

Cycling Adventures in the Tuscan Countryside

Explore the picturesque landscapes of Pisa and its surrounding countryside on two wheels with cycling adventures that cater to riders of all levels. From leisurely rides along scenic countryside roads to challenging mountain bike trails, Pisa offers a diverse range of cycling experiences to suit every preference. Renting a bike for a self-guided tour can cost between €15 to €30 per day, while guided cycling tours with experienced instructors may range from €50 to €100 per person, depending on the duration and level of support provided.

Practical Information and Tips
Before embarking on an adventure sports excursion in Pisa, it's essential to consider a few practicalities. Check the weather forecast and dress accordingly, wearing appropriate clothing and footwear for the activity. Be sure to book your adventure sports experiences in advance, especially during peak tourist seasons, to secure your spot and avoid disappointment. Additionally, always follow the instructions of experienced guides and instructors to ensure a safe and enjoyable experience.

Whether you're scaling limestone cliffs, conquering white-water rapids, or exploring scenic countryside trails, Pisa offers a playground for outdoor enthusiasts and adrenaline junkies alike. With a wide range of adventure sports activities to choose from, visitors can immerse themselves in the natural beauty of Tuscany while indulging in heart-pounding thrills and unforgettable experiences. So, gear up, embrace the spirit of adventure, and embark on an adrenaline-fueled journey through the wild landscapes of Pisa.

8.6 Family and Kids Friendly Activities
Pisa isn't just a destination for history buffs and architecture enthusiasts—it's also a playground for families seeking memorable adventures and quality time together. From exploring historic landmarks to enjoying thrilling attractions, the city offers a diverse array of family-friendly activities that cater to all ages. Let's embark on a journey through Pisa's family-friendly attractions, where laughter, excitement, and joy abound.

Leaning Tower of Pisa: A Timeless Icon for All Ages
No visit to Pisa is complete without marveling at the Leaning Tower, an iconic symbol of the city's rich history and architectural prowess. Families can embark on a guided tour

of the tower, ascending its spiral staircase to reach the top and enjoy panoramic views of Pisa from above. Tickets for climbing the tower cost around €18 for adults and €8 for children aged 8 to 18, with free admission for children under 8. While climbing the tower requires a minimum height restriction of 1.20 meters for safety reasons, younger children can still enjoy exploring the surrounding Piazza dei Miracoli and its fascinating monuments.

Pisa Mural Tondo: A Colorful Artistic Adventure

For a dose of creativity and culture, families can visit the Pisa Mural Tondo, a vibrant outdoor mural located near the city center. Created by local artists, this colorful masterpiece depicts scenes from Pisa's history and showcases the city's artistic spirit. Families can take a leisurely stroll along the mural, admiring the intricate details and vibrant colors while engaging in interactive activities designed for children. Best of all, admission to the Pisa Mural Tondo is free, making it an accessible and enjoyable outing for families of all budgets.

Pisa Aquarium: Dive into the Wonders of the Sea

Immerse yourself in the mesmerizing world of marine life at the Pisa Aquarium, where families can discover a diverse array of aquatic creatures from around the globe. Located within the Cittadella Vecchia complex, the aquarium features interactive exhibits, educational presentations, and hands-on activities for visitors of all ages. Tickets for the Pisa Aquarium cost around €10 for adults and €7 for children aged 4 to 12, with discounts available for families and groups. From colorful tropical fish to majestic sharks, the aquarium offers an unforgettable journey beneath the waves for the whole family to enjoy.

Giardino Scotto

Escape the hustle and bustle of the city and unwind at Giardino Scotto, a scenic park nestled along the banks of the Arno River. Families can enjoy picnicking on lush green lawns, playing on playgrounds, and exploring winding paths that meander through beautiful gardens. Admission to Giardino Scotto is free, making it an ideal spot for families to relax and recharge amidst nature's beauty. Don't forget to bring along a frisbee or soccer ball for some outdoor fun, or simply sit back and enjoy a leisurely afternoon in the sun.

Before embarking on family-friendly activities in Pisa, it's essential to plan ahead and consider a few practicalities. Check the opening hours and ticket prices for each attraction, and consider purchasing tickets online in advance to skip the queues. Bring along snacks, water, sunscreen, and comfortable walking shoes to ensure a comfortable and enjoyable experience for the whole family. Additionally, don't forget to pack a camera to capture precious moments and memories that will last a lifetime.

From scaling the iconic Leaning Tower to exploring vibrant murals and discovering underwater wonders at the aquarium, Pisa offers a wealth of family-friendly activities that promise laughter, learning, and unforgettable adventures. Whether you're admiring historic landmarks, immersing yourself in art and culture, or simply enjoying quality time together in nature's embrace, Pisa invites families to create cherished memories that will be treasured for years to come. So, pack your bags, gather your loved ones, and embark on a journey of discovery and joy in the heart of Tuscany.

8.7 Activities for Solo Travelers

Solo travel offers a unique opportunity for self-discovery, allowing you to explore new destinations at your own pace and on your own terms. In Pisa, solo travelers can immerse themselves in the city's rich history, vibrant culture, and breathtaking landscapes, embarking on unforgettable adventures that promise moments of reflection, inspiration, and personal growth. Let's embark on a journey through Pisa's solo-friendly activities, where the freedom of exploration knows no bounds.

Piazza del Duomo

Begin your journey in Pisa with a leisurely stroll through Piazza del Duomo, the heart of the city's historic center and home to its most iconic landmarks. Marvel at the magnificent Leaning Tower, the stunning Cathedral, and the ornate Baptistery, soaking in the grandeur of these architectural marvels at your own pace. Take your time to admire the intricate details of the sculptures and facades, capturing memorable photos and moments of contemplation amidst the bustling square. While entry to the Cathedral is free, tickets for climbing the Leaning Tower cost around €18, providing solo travelers with the option to explore these historic treasures on their own terms.

Exploring Pisa's Hidden Gems

Venture off the beaten path and discover Pisa's hidden gems, where solo travelers can uncover lesser-known attractions and hidden corners of the city. Explore the charming streets of the San Francesco district, where historic buildings and quaint cafes await around every corner. Wander through the Giardino Scotto, a tranquil oasis along the banks of the Arno River, where you can relax amidst lush greenery and picturesque views. For art enthusiasts, a visit to the Palazzo Blu offers a solo-friendly experience, with rotating exhibitions showcasing contemporary and historical artworks from local and international artists. Admission prices for attractions such as the Palazzo Blu may vary depending on the exhibition, typically ranging from €8 to €12.

Culinary Adventures

Indulge in the culinary delights of Pisa as a solo traveler, sampling the city's renowned Tuscan cuisine at local trattorias and osterias. Treat yourself to a solo dining experience at Osteria dei Cavalieri, where you can savor traditional dishes such as ribollita, pappa al pomodoro, and bistecca alla fiorentina in a cozy and welcoming atmosphere. For a taste of Pisa's street food scene, head to the bustling Mercato delle Vettovaglie, where vendors offer a variety of local specialties, including lampredotto sandwiches, panini with porchetta, and fritto misto seafood. Prices for meals at local restaurants and markets can vary depending on the dish and venue, with options available to suit every budget.

Practical Information and Tips

Before embarking on solo adventures in Pisa, it's essential to plan ahead and consider a few practicalities. Familiarize yourself with the city's public transportation system, including buses and trains, to navigate your way around Pisa with ease. Consider investing in a city pass or guided walking tour to maximize your time and gain insights into the city's history and culture. Bring along a map or download offline navigation apps to help you navigate the streets and discover hidden gems. Additionally, be open to meeting fellow travelers and locals along the way, as solo travel offers the opportunity for meaningful connections and shared experiences.

Solo travel in Pisa offers a wealth of opportunities for self-discovery, adventure, and cultural immersion. Whether you're wandering through historic landmarks, exploring hidden corners of the city, or indulging in gastronomic delights, solo travelers can embrace the freedom of exploration and create unforgettable memories in the heart of Tuscany. So, pack your bags, set out on your solo adventure, and let Pisa inspire you with its beauty, history, and warmth of hospitality.

CHAPTER 9
SHOPPING IN PISA

Click the link or Scan QR Code with a device to view a comprehensive map of Shopping Options in Pisa – *https://shorturl.at/aimqT*

9.1 Local Markets and Street Vendors

One of the best ways to experience the authentic flavors and vibrant atmosphere of Pisa is by exploring its bustling markets and street vendors. From fresh produce to artisanal crafts, these local hubs offer a glimpse into the city's rich culinary heritage and artisanal traditions. Join me as we embark on a journey through six of Pisa's most beloved markets and street vendors, where the sights, sounds, and smells will tantalize your senses and leave you craving for more.

Mercato delle Vettovaglie

Located in the heart of Pisa's historic center, the Mercato delle Vettovaglie is a food lover's paradise, brimming with fresh produce, gourmet delicacies, and local specialties. While wandering through the market's lively stalls, you'll encounter a variety of vibrant fruits and vegetables, aromatic herbs and spices, and artisanal cheeses and cured meats. Don't miss the chance to sample traditional Tuscan dishes from the market's numerous street food vendors, offering treats such as lampredotto sandwiches, panini with porchetta, and freshly baked focaccia. Prices at the Mercato delle Vettovaglie vary depending on the vendor and product, but you can expect to find affordable options to suit every budget.

Piazza delle Vettovaglie

Adjacent to the Mercato delle Vettovaglie, Piazza delle Vettovaglie is a bustling square lined with charming cafes, lively bars, and quaint street vendors. Here, you can mingle with locals as you browse through stalls selling artisanal crafts, handmade jewelry, and unique souvenirs.Indulge in a freshly brewed espresso or a refreshing Aperol Spritz at one of the square's al fresco cafes, and immerse yourself in the lively atmosphere while street performers entertain passersby with music and dance. While prices may vary depending on the vendor and product, bargaining is not typically practiced at Piazza delle Vettovaglie.

San Zeno Market

For vintage enthusiasts and collectors, the San Zeno Market is a must-visit destination in Pisa. Located in the San Zeno neighborhood, this eclectic flea market offers a diverse array of antiques, collectibles, and one-of-a-kind treasures waiting to be discovered. From retro clothing and vinyl records to antique furniture and rare books, you'll find an eclectic mix of items that reflect Pisa's rich cultural heritage. Prices at the San Zeno Market can vary widely depending on the rarity and condition of the items, so be prepared to haggle and negotiate with vendors to secure the best deals.

Sant'Antonio Market

Located along the Arno River, the Sant'Antonio Market is a lively outdoor market bursting with the sights, sounds, and aromas of local vendors and artisans. Here, you'll discover a diverse array of fresh produce, artisanal cheeses, and homemade pastries., as well as handcrafted goods such as leather goods, pottery, and textiles. Take a leisurely stroll along the market's waterfront promenade, sampling local delicacies and soaking in the picturesque views of the river and surrounding landmarks. Prices at the Sant'Antonio Market are generally reasonable, and visitors can expect to find affordable options for food and souvenirs.

Pisa Vintage Market

For a blast from the past, head to the Pisa Vintage Market, where you'll find a treasure trove of retro clothing, accessories, and memorabilia from decades past. Located in the San Martino district, this lively market showcases the best of vintage fashion and nostalgia, with vendors offering everything from 1950s dresses and vinyl records to antique cameras and classic toys. Prices at the Pisa Vintage Market vary depending on the rarity and condition of the items, but visitors can expect to find unique bargains and hidden gems that evoke the glamour and nostalgia of bygone eras.

Tips for Visitors

When visiting Pisa's markets and street vendors, it's essential to come prepared with cash, as many vendors may not accept credit cards. Be sure to bring along a reusable shopping bag to carry your purchases and consider wearing comfortable shoes for walking and exploring. While bargaining is not common at all markets, it's always worth negotiating for a better price, especially when purchasing multiple items or larger quantities. Lastly, don't forget to engage with vendors and locals, as they can offer valuable insights and recommendations for experiencing the best of Pisa's local culture and cuisine.

Exploring Pisa's markets and street vendors is a feast for the senses, offering visitors the opportunity to sample local delicacies, discover unique treasures, and immerse themselves in the city's vibrant culture and heritage. Whether you're browsing for fresh produce at the Mercato delle Vettovaglie, hunting for vintage finds at the Pisa Vintage Market, or simply soaking in the lively atmosphere of Piazza delle Vettovaglie, each market and street vendor offers a unique and memorable experience that will leave you enchanted and inspired by the flavors and flair of Pisa.

9.2 Souvenir Shops and Artisanal Crafts

Souvenir shops and artisanal craft stores in Pisa offer visitors a chance to take home a piece of the city's rich cultural heritage. From handcrafted leather goods to intricate ceramics and traditional Tuscan delicacies, these stores showcase the talent and creativity of local artisans, providing an opportunity to support the local economy while finding unique mementos to cherish. Let's delve into the world of Pisa's souvenir shops and artisanal crafts, where every purchase tells a story of craftsmanship, tradition, and creativity.

Bottega dei Filati

Located in the heart of Pisa's historic center, Bottega dei Filati is a charming yarn shop that caters to knitting enthusiasts and textile artists. Here, visitors can browse a wide selection of high-quality yarns, needles, and accessories, sourced from local Italian producers as well as international brands. Whether you're a seasoned knitter or a novice crafter, the knowledgeable staff at Bottega dei Filati are always on hand to offer advice and recommendations. Prices for yarn and knitting supplies vary depending on the brand and quality, with options available to suit every budget.

Artefatti d'Arte

Artefatti d'Arte is a boutique gallery located near Piazza dei Miracoli, dedicated to showcasing the finest examples of Tuscan craftsmanship and artisanal traditions. Visitors to Artefatti d'Arte can explore a curated collection of handmade ceramics, glassware, textiles, and jewelry, each piece crafted with meticulous attention to detail and a passion for preserving local heritage. Whether you're searching for a unique gift or a statement piece for your home, Artefatti d'Arte offers a treasure trove of artistic treasures to discover. Prices for artisanal crafts at Artefatti d'Arte vary depending on the artist and materials used, with options available to suit every taste and budget.

La Bottega del Mosaico

For a truly unique souvenir from Pisa, look no further than La Bottega del Mosaico, a boutique studio specializing in handmade mosaic artworks. Located in the San Francesco district, this charming shop offers visitors the opportunity to watch skilled artisans at work as they create intricate mosaic designs using traditional techniques and locally sourced materials. From small decorative pieces to larger-scale artworks, La Bottega del Mosaico showcases the beauty and versatility of mosaic art, with prices varying depending on the size and complexity of the piece.

Tips for Visitors

When exploring Pisa's souvenir shops and artisanal craft stores, it's essential to take your time and browse at leisure, allowing yourself to fully appreciate the skill and creativity behind each handmade item. Consider purchasing souvenirs directly from local artisans whenever possible, as this ensures that your support goes directly to the creators themselves.Don't hesitate to ask questions and interact with shop owners and artisans, as they can provide valuable insights into the craftsmanship and cultural importance of their creations. Lastly, remember to pack your souvenirs carefully to ensure they arrive home safely and serve as lasting reminders of your time in Pisa.

Exploring Pisa's souvenir shops and artisanal craft stores is an opportunity to immerse yourself in the city's rich cultural heritage and take home a piece of its timeless charm. Whether you're admiring handcrafted ceramics, browsing through exquisite textiles, or marveling at intricate mosaic artworks, each souvenir tells a story of tradition, craftsmanship, and creativity. So, take a stroll through Pisa's cobblestone streets, discover hidden gems in its boutique shops, and let the city's artisanal treasures inspire you to create memories that will last a lifetime.

9.3 Fashion Boutiques and Designer Stores

Pisa's fashion boutiques and designer stores offer visitors a unique shopping experience that seamlessly blends contemporary style with traditional craftsmanship. Situated among the city's charming streets, these boutique shops exhibit the latest trends in Italian fashion while honoring the country's rich sartorial legacy, From high-end designer labels to locally crafted accessories, each store tells a story of artistry, elegance, and timeless sophistication. Join me as we embark on a journey through Pisa's fashion scene, where every purchase is a celebration of style and culture.

La Bottega del Tintoretto

Located near Piazza dei Miracoli, La Bottega del Tintoretto is a renowned fashion boutique known for its curated selection of high-quality clothing and accessories. Here, visitors can browse through racks of elegant dresses, tailored suits, and chic separates, each carefully chosen for its timeless style and impeccable craftsmanship. Whether you're searching for the perfect outfit for a special occasion or simply looking to update your wardrobe with classic pieces, La Bottega del Tintoretto offers an array of options to suit every taste and occasion. Prices at the boutique vary depending on the designer and garment, with options available to accommodate different budgets.

Atelier Emilio Pucci

For a taste of Italian glamour and luxury, head to Atelier Emilio Pucci, located in the heart of Pisa's fashion district. This iconic designer store showcases the latest collections from the renowned fashion house, known for its bold prints, vibrant colors, and effortless elegance. From flowing silk dresses to tailored blazers and statement accessories, Atelier Emilio Pucci offers visitors the chance to indulge in the brand's signature style and sophistication. Prices at the boutique reflect the designer label's prestige, with garments and accessories available at various price points to cater to different budgets.

Boutique dei Fiori

Tucked away in a charming alley near the Arno River, Boutique dei Fiori is a hidden gem known for its whimsical aesthetic and bohemian-inspired fashion. Here, visitors can explore racks of flowing dresses, floral prints, and artisanal accessories, each reflecting the boutique's eclectic and romantic vibe. Whether you're in search of a breezy summer dress or a unique statement piece to add to your wardrobe, Boutique dei Fiori offers a selection of clothing and accessories that exude laid-back elegance and charm. Prices at the boutique are generally affordable, with options available for those seeking stylish pieces without breaking the bank.

Tips for Visitors

When exploring Pisa's fashion boutiques and designer stores, it's essential to dress comfortably and wear appropriate footwear for walking and browsing. Take your time to explore each store and don't hesitate to ask for assistance or recommendations from the knowledgeable staff. Consider shopping during off-peak hours to avoid crowds and enjoy a more relaxed shopping experience. Lastly, don't forget to bring along a reusable shopping bag to carry your purchases and minimize waste.

From classic elegance to bohemian chic, Pisa's fashion boutiques and designer stores offer visitors a glimpse into the vibrant world of Italian style and sophistication. Whether you're searching for a timeless wardrobe staple or a statement piece to elevate your look, these boutique shops provide a curated selection of clothing and accessories that celebrate the artistry and craftsmanship of Italian fashion. So, immerse yourself in Pisa's fashion scene, discover hidden gems in its boutique shops, and let your style journey through the city be a reflection of your own unique taste and personality.

9.4 Specialty Food Stores and Delicatessens

The culinary landscape of Pisa mirrors the city's abundant cultural heritage and gastronomic traditions. From authentic Tuscan tastes to gourmet delights, specialty food stores and delicatessens in Pisa invite visitors to embark on a culinary adventure through the region's finest ingredients and culinary innovations.

Antica Salumeria Buonamici

Located in the heart of Pisa's historic center, Antica Salumeria Buonamici is a beloved institution known for its exquisite selection of Italian charcuterie, cheeses, and gourmet specialties. Here, visitors can browse through shelves laden with cured meats, aged cheeses, and artisanal products sourced from the finest producers across Italy. Whether you're craving a platter of prosciutto and pecorino or in search of the perfect accompaniment for your antipasto spread, Antica Salumeria Buonamici offers an unparalleled selection of authentic Italian delicacies. Prices at the delicatessen vary depending on the product and quality, with options available to suit every budget.

Emporio del Gusto

Emporio del Gusto is a culinary haven located near the Arno River, offering visitors an immersive experience in the world of Italian gastronomy. This gourmet store boasts an extensive range of artisanal products, including olive oils, balsamic vinegars, pasta, sauces, and sweets, sourced from small-scale producers and local artisans. Visitors to Emporio del Gusto can explore the store's carefully curated selection, sample specialty products, and receive personalized recommendations from the knowledgeable staff.

Whether you're a seasoned chef or a culinary enthusiast, Emporio del Gusto is sure to delight your taste buds and inspire your culinary creations. Prices at the store vary depending on the product and brand, with options available for every budget and palate.

Mercato delle Vettovaglie

For a taste of Pisa's vibrant market scene, head to Mercato delle Vettovaglie, a bustling food market located in the historic center of the city. Here, visitors can envelop themselves in the sights, sounds, and aromas of Italian cuisine, as they wander through stalls brimming with fresh produce, seafood, meats, cheeses, and more. From seasonal fruits and vegetables to locally caught fish and regional specialties, Mercato delle Vettovaglie offers a feast for the senses and a glimpse into the daily life of Pisa's residents. Prices at the market vary depending on the product and vendor, with opportunities to haggle and find bargains for savvy shoppers.

Tips for Visitors

When exploring specialty food stores and delicatessens in Pisa, take the time to savor the flavors and sample the local specialties. Engage with shop owners and staff to learn more about the products and their culinary significance, and don't be afraid to ask for recommendations or cooking tips. Consider purchasing edible souvenirs to bring home a taste of Pisa's gastronomic heritage, whether it's a jar of locally made pesto or a bottle of artisanal olive oil. Lastly, embrace the opportunity to indulge in the simple pleasures of Italian cuisine and let your taste buds guide you on a delicious journey through Pisa's culinary landscape.

Specialty food stores and delicatessens in Pisa offer visitors a window into the region's rich culinary heritage and a chance to discover the flavors that define Italian cuisine. From artisanal charcuterie and cheeses to gourmet pantry staples and fresh produce, these culinary destinations provide a feast for the senses and an opportunity to immerse oneself in the gastronomic delights of Pisa. So, whether you're exploring the cobblestone streets of the historic center or browsing the stalls of the local market, let your culinary adventure in Pisa be a celebration of flavor, tradition, and the joy of good food.

9.5 Shopping Districts and Malls

Pisa's shopping districts and malls offer visitors a diverse array of retail experiences, blending modern convenience with traditional charm. From bustling pedestrian streets lined with boutique shops to contemporary malls housing international brands, exploring Pisa's shopping scene is a delightful journey that combines retail therapy with cultural exploration. Join me as we venture through the city's vibrant shopping districts and discover the treasures that await around every corner.

Corso Italia

Corso Italia stands as one of Pisa's most iconic shopping streets, attracting locals and tourists alike with its bustling atmosphere and diverse array of stores. Stretching from Piazza Vittorio Emanuele II to Piazza delle Vettovaglie, this pedestrian-friendly thoroughfare is lined with shops selling everything from fashion and accessories to artisanal crafts and souvenirs. Visitors can browse through boutique stores, designer labels, and local artisans, immersing themselves in the vibrant energy of Pisa's retail scene. Whether you're hunting for the perfect Italian leather shoes or searching for unique gifts to bring back home, Corso Italia offers a shopping experience that combines style, variety, and authenticity.

Piazza dei Cavalieri

Nestled within the historic heart of Pisa, Piazza dei Cavalieri is not only a cultural landmark but also a hub for unique shopping experiences. Here, visitors can explore quaint alleyways and hidden courtyards that are home to artisan workshops, antique stores, and specialty boutiques. From handcrafted jewelry and vintage treasures to locally made ceramics and textiles, Piazza dei Cavalieri offers a glimpse into Pisa's artisanal heritage and creative spirit. As you wander through the cobblestone streets of this historic square, allow yourself to be enchanted by the charm and authenticity of the shops that line its picturesque lanes.

Le Corte

For those seeking a more contemporary shopping experience, Le Corte provides a haven of modernity and convenience in the heart of Pisa. This sleek and stylish mall boasts a diverse range of stores, including international fashion brands, electronics retailers, and gourmet food outlets. Visitors can indulge in a spot of retail therapy, browse the latest trends, and enjoy a variety of dining options all under one roof. With ample parking facilities and easy access from the city center, Le Corte offers a hassle-free shopping experience that caters to both locals and tourists alike.

Tips for Visitors

When exploring Pisa's shopping districts and malls, it's helpful to wear comfortable footwear and dress for the weather, as you may be doing a fair amount of walking outdoors. Take your time to explore each store and don't hesitate to ask for assistance or recommendations from the friendly staff. Consider visiting during off-peak hours to avoid crowds and enjoy a more relaxed shopping experience. Lastly, don't forget to bring along a reusable shopping bag to carry your purchases and minimize waste.

Whether you're strolling down the historic streets of Corso Italia, uncovering hidden treasures in Piazza dei Cavalieri, or indulging in modern retail therapy at Le Corte, exploring Pisa's shopping districts and malls is a journey filled with discovery and delight. From timeless fashion finds to artisanal crafts and gourmet treats, each shopping destination offers a unique glimpse into the city's culture, creativity, and commerce. So, immerse yourself in the joy of shopping, embrace the diversity of Pisa's retail landscape, and let your retail adventures be a memorable part of your visit to this enchanting city.

CHAPTER 10

DAY TRIPS AND EXCURSIONS

10.1 Florence: The Cradle of the Renaissance

Embarking on a day trip from Pisa to Florence offers visitors the opportunity to immerse themselves in the cultural richness and artistic splendor of one of Italy's most iconic cities. Known as the Cradle of the Renaissance, Florence boasts a treasure trove of architectural marvels, world-class museums, and timeless artworks that continue to captivate travelers from around the globe. Join me as we embark on a journey to Florence, where every street corner tells a story and every masterpiece beckons with its beauty and brilliance.

Journeying from Pisa to Florence

Traveling from Pisa to Florence is a seamless and convenient experience, with various transportation options available to suit different preferences and budgets. Visitors can opt to travel by train, with frequent and efficient services departing from Pisa Centrale station and arriving at Florence's Santa Maria Novella station in approximately one hour. Alternatively, private shuttle services and guided tours offer a hassle-free way to explore Florence's highlights with the added convenience of door-to-door transportation.

Exploring Florence's Cultural Heritage

Upon arriving in Florence, visitors are greeted by a cityscape steeped in history and culture, with architectural wonders awaiting around every corner. A visit to the iconic Florence Cathedral, with its magnificent dome designed by Brunelleschi provides a glimpse into the city's architectural mastery and religious heritage. Nearby, the Uffizi Gallery beckons art enthusiasts with its unparalleled collection of Renaissance masterpieces, including works by Michelangelo, Leonardo da Vinci, and Botticelli.

Strolling Through Florence's Historic Center

One of the highlights of a day trip to Florence is simply wandering through the city's historic center, where narrow cobblestone streets lead to charming piazzas, bustling markets, and artisan workshops. Visitors can explore the picturesque Ponte Vecchio bridge, lined with jewelers and boutiques, or marvel at the grandeur of the Palazzo Vecchio in Piazza della Signoria. Along the way, gelaterias, trattorias, and cafes beckon with tempting treats and authentic Tuscan cuisine, inviting visitors to savor the flavors of Florence.

Immersing in Florence's Artistic Legacy

No visit to Florence is complete without delving into its rich artistic legacy, which spans centuries of creativity and innovation. In addition to the Uffizi Gallery, art enthusiasts can explore the Accademia Gallery, home to Michelangelo's iconic statue of David, or wander through the Boboli Gardens, a verdant oasis of Renaissance beauty. For those seeking a deeper understanding of Florence's history and culture, guided tours and audio guides offer insightful commentary and behind-the-scenes access to the city's most renowned landmarks.

A day trip from Pisa to Florence promises an unforgettable adventure filled with art, history, and timeless beauty. Whether marveling at Michelangelo's masterpieces, savoring the flavors of Tuscan cuisine, or simply soaking in the ambiance of Florence's historic streets, visitors are sure to be captivated by the city's charm and allure. So, pack your camera, lace up your walking shoes, and prepare to be enchanted by the Cradle of the Renaissance on a day trip from Pisa to Florence.

10.2 Lucca: Medieval Charm and City Walls

Embarking on a day trip from Pisa to Lucca offers visitors the opportunity to step back in time and explore the medieval charm of one of Tuscany's hidden gems. With its well-preserved city walls, cobblestone streets, and Renaissance architecture, Lucca beckons travelers with its timeless allure and rich cultural heritage. Join me as we venture from Pisa to Lucca, where every corner reveals a story waiting to be told.

Journeying from Pisa to Lucca

Traveling from Pisa to Lucca is a straightforward journey, with several transportation options available to suit different preferences. Visitors can opt to take a short train ride from Pisa Centrale station to Lucca, with trains departing regularly throughout the day and offering a comfortable and efficient way to reach the city. Alternatively, guided tours and private transfers provide a convenient option for those seeking a more personalized and hassle-free experience.

Walking the Historic Walls

One of the highlights of a day trip to Lucca is walking along the city's historic walls, which encircle the old town and offer panoramic views of the surrounding countryside. Built in the Renaissance era, the walls provide a picturesque backdrop for leisurely strolls and scenic bike rides, inviting visitors to immerse themselves in Lucca's rich history and architectural beauty. Along the way, charming gardens, cafes, and historic landmarks await, offering opportunities for relaxation and exploration.

Exploring Lucca's Architectural Treasures

Lucca boasts a wealth of architectural treasures, from medieval towers and Romanesque churches to elegant palaces and Renaissance squares. Visitors can wander through the winding streets of the old town, admiring the well-preserved facades and hidden courtyards that reveal the city's past. Must-see landmarks include the Cathedral of San Martino, with its intricate marble facade and stunning artworks, and the Guinigi Tower, crowned with oak trees and offering panoramic views of Lucca's skyline.

Immersing in Cultural Delights

In addition to its architectural wonders, Lucca offers a wealth of cultural experiences for visitors to enjoy. Art enthusiasts can explore the city's museums and galleries, which showcase a diverse range of artworks spanning centuries of creativity. Meanwhile, food lovers can sample local delicacies at bustling markets and trattorias, where traditional Tuscan flavors take center stage. For a taste of Lucca's vibrant culture, be sure to visit the Piazza dell'Anfiteatro, a charming square built on the site of an ancient Roman amphitheater and bustling with life.

A day trip from Pisa to Lucca promises an enchanting journey through time, where medieval charm and Renaissance splendor converge in a picturesque setting. Whether strolling along the historic walls, exploring architectural treasures, or immersing in cultural delights, visitors are sure to be captivated by Lucca's timeless allure and warm hospitality. So, pack your sense of adventure and embark on a memorable day trip from Pisa to Lucca, where every moment promises discovery and delight.

10.3 Cinque Terre: Coastal Beauty and Hiking Trails

Embarking on a day trip from Pisa to Cinque Terre promises a journey of breathtaking coastal beauty, charming fishing villages, and scenic hiking trails. Perched along the rugged coastline of the Italian Riviera, Cinque Terre captivates visitors with its vibrant houses, crystal-clear waters, and terraced vineyards. Join me as we venture from Pisa to Cinque Terre, where each village tells a story and every vista takes your breath away.

Journeying from Pisa to Cinque Terre

Traveling from Pisa to Cinque Terre is a seamless experience, with various transportation options available to suit different preferences. Visitors can opt to travel by train, with regular services departing from Pisa Centrale station and arriving at the villages of Cinque Terre in approximately two hours. Alternatively, guided tours and private transfers offer a convenient way to explore Cinque Terre's highlights with the added flexibility of personalized itineraries and expert local guides.

Exploring the Five Villages

Cinque Terre is comprised of five picturesque villages – Monterosso al Mare, Vernazza, Corniglia, Manarola, and Riomaggiore – each boasting its own unique character and charm. Visitors can spend the day wandering through narrow cobblestone streets, admiring pastel-colored houses adorned with vibrant flowers, and soaking in the laid-back atmosphere of coastal life. Along the way, quaint harbors, rocky coves, and panoramic viewpoints offer endless opportunities for exploration and discovery.

Hiking Trails and Scenic Routes

One of the highlights of a day trip to Cinque Terre is hiking along the network of scenic trails that connect the five villages, offering breathtaking views of the coastline and surrounding countryside. The famous Sentiero Azzurro (Blue Trail) winds its way along the cliffs, passing through vineyards, olive groves, and terraced hillsides, providing hikers with a glimpse into the region's agricultural heritage. For those seeking a more challenging adventure, the high-altitude trails offer panoramic vistas and secluded beaches, rewarding hikers with unforgettable experiences amidst nature's beauty.

Savoring Local Flavors

No visit to Cinque Terre is complete without savoring the region's culinary delights, which reflect the bounty of the sea and the richness of the land. Visitors can sample fresh seafood dishes, such as anchovies marinated in olive oil, or indulge in Ligurian specialties like pesto pasta and focaccia bread. Meanwhile, local vineyards produce crisp white wines, such as Sciacchetrà and Vermentino, which pair perfectly with the flavors of Cinque Terre's cuisine. For a true taste of the region, be sure to visit family-run trattorias and seaside cafes, where warm hospitality and authentic flavors await.

A day trip from Pisa to Cinque Terre promises an unforgettable journey through coastal splendor, where rugged cliffs, charming villages, and scenic trails converge in a breathtaking landscape. Whether hiking along coastal paths, savoring local flavors, or simply soaking in the laid-back atmosphere of village life, visitors are sure to be captivated by Cinque Terre's timeless allure and natural beauty. So, pack your hiking shoes, bring your sense of adventure, and embark on a day trip from Pisa to Cinque Terre, where every moment promises discovery and delight.

10.4 Siena: Gothic Architecture and Palio Festival

A day trip from Pisa to Siena offers visitors the chance to immerse themselves in the rich history, Gothic architecture, and vibrant culture of one of Tuscany's most captivating cities. Renowned for its medieval charm, iconic landmarks, and the world-famous Palio Festival, Siena beckons travelers with its timeless allure and captivating beauty. Join me as we embark on a journey from Pisa to Siena, where every corner reveals a piece of Italy's illustrious past.

Journeying from Pisa to Siena

Traveling from Pisa to Siena is a straightforward journey, with several transportation options available to suit different preferences. Visitors can opt to travel by train, with regular services departing from Pisa Centrale station and arriving at Siena's central station in approximately two hours. Alternatively, guided tours and private transfers offer a convenient and customizable way to explore Siena's highlights with the expertise of local guides.

Exploring Siena's Gothic Architecture

Siena is renowned for its Gothic architecture, with the majestic Cathedral of Santa Maria Assunta standing as a testament to the city's artistic and cultural heritage. Visitors can marvel at the intricate facade adorned with sculptural masterpieces, venture inside to admire the breathtaking interior, and climb to the top of the cathedral's tower for panoramic views of the city and surrounding countryside. Other architectural treasures include the Palazzo Pubblico, with its iconic Torre del Mangia, and the historic Piazza del Campo, a UNESCO World Heritage Site and the heart of Siena's civic life.

Immersing in Siena's Cultural Heritage

No visit to Siena is complete without experiencing the world-famous Palio di Siena, a historic horse race that takes place twice a year in the heart of the city's historic center. Dating back to the Middle Ages, the Palio is a thrilling spectacle of pageantry, tradition, and fierce competition, where rival contrade (neighborhoods) compete for victory in a heart-pounding race around the Piazza del Campo. Beyond the Palio, visitors can explore Siena's rich cultural heritage through its museums, art galleries, and historic landmarks, which offer insights into the city's illustrious past and vibrant present.

Indulging in Tuscan Cuisine

Siena's culinary scene is as rich and diverse as its cultural heritage, with traditional trattorias, family-run osterias, and gourmet restaurants offering a tantalizing array of Tuscan dishes and local specialties. Visitors can savor regional favorites such as pici pasta with wild boar ragu, ribollita (Tuscan bread soup), and panforte (a dense, fruitcake-like dessert). For an authentic taste of Siena, be sure to explore the city's bustling markets, where fresh produce, artisanal cheeses, and local wines tempt the taste buds and delight the senses.

A day trip from Pisa to Siena promises an unforgettable journey through Gothic splendor, cultural heritage, and timeless traditions. Whether marveling at architectural wonders, witnessing the excitement of the Palio Festival, or indulging in Tuscan cuisine, visitors are sure to be captivated by Siena's charm and allure. So, pack your sense of adventure, bring your appetite, and embark on a day trip from Pisa to Siena, where every moment promises discovery and delight in the heart of Tuscany.

10.5 Livorno: Port City and Maritime History

A day trip from Pisa to Livorno offers travelers a chance to delve into the rich maritime history, vibrant cultural scene, and coastal charm of this bustling port city. Situated along the scenic shores of the Ligurian Sea, Livorno beckons visitors with its bustling harbor, historic landmarks, and vibrant waterfront promenades. Join me as we embark on a journey from Pisa to Livorno, where the sea has shaped the city's identity and culture for centuries.

Journeying from Pisa to Livorno

Traveling from Pisa to Livorno is a straightforward journey, with various transportation options available to suit different preferences. Visitors can opt to travel by train, with frequent services departing from Pisa Centrale station and arriving at Livorno Centrale station in approximately 20-30 minutes. Alternatively, guided tours and private transfers offer a convenient and customizable way to explore Livorno's highlights with the expertise of local guides.

Exploring Livorno's Maritime Heritage

Livorno's history is deeply intertwined with its maritime heritage, and visitors can explore the city's seafaring legacy at its bustling harbor and waterfront promenades. The Porto Mediceo, built by the Medici family in the 16th century, serves as the heart of Livorno's maritime activity, with bustling docks, fishing boats, and waterfront cafes creating a lively atmosphere. Nearby, the Naval Academy and Maritime Museum offer insights into Livorno's naval history, showcasing ship models, artifacts, and exhibits that highlight the city's maritime traditions.

Discovering Livorno's Architectural Treasures

Livorno boasts a rich architectural heritage, with historic churches, elegant squares, and grand palaces that reflect the city's cultural diversity and cosmopolitan flair. Visitors can wander through the picturesque streets of Livorno's Old Town, where Renaissance and Baroque buildings mingle with neoclassical facades and hidden courtyards. Highlights include the Cathedral of Livorno, with its striking dome and ornate interior, and the Piazza della Repubblica, a vibrant square lined with cafes, shops, and historic buildings.

Indulging in Livorno's Culinary Delights
No visit to Livorno is complete without savoring its culinary delights, which showcase the region's bounty of fresh seafood, artisanal products, and traditional recipes. Visitors can sample local specialties such as cacciucco (a hearty fish stew), frittura di pesce (fried seafood platter), and torta di ceci (chickpea flour pancake), which are served at traditional trattorias, seafood shacks, and street food stalls throughout the city. Meanwhile, Livorno's vibrant Mercato Centrale offers a feast for the senses, with stalls piled high with fresh produce, fish, meats, cheeses, and other local delicacies.

Relaxing on Livorno's Coastal Promenades and Beaches
Livorno's scenic waterfront promenades and sandy beaches provide the perfect backdrop for relaxation and leisure activities. Visitors can stroll along the Terrazza Mascagni, a picturesque seafront promenade adorned with elegant black and white checkered tiles and lined with benches, cafes, and panoramic views of the sea. Nearby, the Medicean Docks offer a tranquil retreat, with scenic walking paths, shady trees, and views of the harbor and coastline. For those seeking sun and sand, Livorno's sandy beaches, such as Cala del Leone and Cala del Sale, offer opportunities for swimming, sunbathing, and water sports amidst stunning coastal scenery.

A day trip from Pisa to Livorno promises an unforgettable journey through maritime history, cultural heritage, and coastal charm.Whether delving into historic landmarks, savoring culinary delights, or simply enjoying the sea breeze alongLivorno's scenic waterfront, visitors are sure to be captivated by the city's timeless allure and vibrant spirit. So, pack your sense of adventure, bring your appetite, and embark on a day trip from Pisa to Livorno, where every moment promises discovery and delight on the shores of the Ligurian Sea.

CHAPTER 11

ENTERTAINMENT AND NIGHTLIFE

11.1 Restaurants: Gastronomic Experiences

Click the link or Scan QR Code with a device to view a comprehensive map of various Restaurants in Pisa – https://shorturl.at/rsEJK

Embarking on a culinary adventure in Pisa offers visitors a delightful exploration of Tuscan cuisine amidst the city's historic ambiance and charming streets. From traditional trattorias to modern bistros, Pisa's restaurant scene caters to every palate, offering a tantalizing array of flavors and culinary experiences. Join me as we discover some of the finest dining establishments that Pisa has to offer.

Trattoria La Buca: Authentic Tuscan Fare
Nestled in the heart of Pisa's historic center, Trattoria La Buca welcomes guests with its cozy ambiance and authentic Tuscan cuisine. Here, visitors can savor classic dishes such as ribollita, pappa al pomodoro, and bistecca alla fiorentina, all made with locally sourced ingredients and prepared with care. The restaurant's extensive wine list features a selection of Tuscan wines, perfect for pairing with the flavorful dishes. Trattoria La Buca is open for lunch and dinner, providing an ideal setting for a memorable dining experience.

Osteria dei Cavalieri: Gastronomic Excellence
Situated near the iconic Leaning Tower, Osteria dei Cavalieri is renowned for its gastronomic excellence and warm hospitality. This charming restaurant offers a sophisticated menu that showcases the best of Tuscan and Italian cuisine, with a focus on seasonal ingredients and creative flair. From handmade pasta dishes to fresh

seafood specialties, every dish at Osteria dei Cavalieri is a culinary masterpiece. Guests can enjoy lunch or dinner in the elegant dining room or al fresco on the picturesque terrace, overlooking Pisa's historic landmarks.

Ristorante Galileo: Modern Italian Cuisine

For a taste of modern Italian cuisine, look no further than Ristorante Galileo. Located in the vibrant San Francesco district, this stylish restaurant offers innovative dishes inspired by traditional recipes, prepared with a contemporary twist. Guests can choose from a diverse menu featuring antipasti, homemade pastas, and inventive meat and fish dishes, all showcasing the chef's creativity and passion for culinary excellence. Ristorante Galileo is open for lunch and dinner, providing an elegant setting for a memorable dining experience in Pisa.

Il Montino: Family-friendly Atmosphere

Il Montino is a family-friendly restaurant located just a short stroll from the Arno River, offering a relaxed atmosphere and hearty Italian fare. The restaurant's menu features a variety of pizzas, pastas, and grilled meats, as well as a selection of vegetarian and vegan options to cater to all dietary preferences. With its welcoming ambiance and attentive service, Il Montino is the perfect spot for a casual meal with family and friends. The restaurant is open throughout the day, making it a convenient choice for both lunch and dinner.

Ristorante La Grotta: Romantic Dining Experience

Nestled in a historic building in the heart of Pisa's medieval quarter, Ristorante La Grotta offers a romantic dining experience amidst ancient stone arches and candlelit tables. The restaurant specializes in Tuscan and seafood cuisine, with an emphasis on fresh, locally sourced ingredients and authentic flavors. Guests can choose from an array of beautifully presented dishes, accompanied by a curated selection of wines from the region. With its intimate ambiance and attentive service, Ristorante La Grotta is the perfect choice for a special occasion or romantic evening out.

From traditional trattorias to modern bistros, Pisa's restaurant scene offers a diverse range of dining experiences to suit every taste and occasion. Whether savoring authentic Tuscan fare at Trattoria La Buca, indulging in gastronomic delights at Osteria dei Cavalieri, or enjoying a romantic dinner at Ristorante La Grotta, visitors are sure to delight in the flavors and ambiance of Pisa's dining establishments. So, immerse yourself in the culinary delights of Pisa and experience the rich gastronomic heritage of this charming city.

11.2 Bars and Pubs: Local Hangouts

Click the link or Scan QR Code with a device to view a comprehensive map of various Bars and Pubs in Pisa – https://shorturl.at/hoqzG

Pisa's bar scene offers a vibrant and eclectic mix of establishments, ranging from historic pubs to trendy cocktail bars, where visitors can unwind and savor the local atmosphere. Whether you're in search of a classic Italian aperitivo, live music, or a cozy spot to enjoy a craft beer, Pisa has something for everyone. Join me as we explore six of the city's most inviting bars and pubs, each with its own unique charm and character.

La Tana del Gatto

Nestled in a historic building near Piazza dei Cavalieri, La Tana del Gatto exudes a cozy and intimate ambiance, making it the perfect spot for a relaxed evening with friends. The bar offers an extensive selection of wines, cocktails, and craft beers, along with a tempting menu of artisanal snacks and small plates. Guests can unwind in the rustic interior or enjoy al fresco seating on the charming outdoor terrace. La Tana del Gatto is open until late, making it an ideal destination for a nightcap or leisurely drinks.

The Lions Fountain

Located in the heart of Pisa's historic center, The Lions Fountain is a beloved British-style pub that brings a taste of England to Tuscany. With its traditional decor, friendly atmosphere, and wide selection of beers on tap, The Lions Fountain offers a quintessential pub experience. Visitors can enjoy a pint of their favorite ale while watching live sports on the big screen or participating in pub quizzes and trivia nights. The pub also serves classic pub fare, including fish and chips, burgers, and hearty pies. Open until late, The Lions Fountain is a popular spot for both locals and visitors alike.

Old Scool

Situated in the San Francesco district, Old Scool is a retro-themed bar that pays homage to the golden age of rock and roll. Decked out with vintage decor, neon signs, and nostalgic memorabilia, the bar transports guests back in time to the 1950s and 60s. Patrons can sip on classic cocktails, enjoy live music performances, or challenge friends to a game of pinball or foosball. With its laid-back atmosphere and friendly staff, Old Scool is a must-visit destination for music lovers and retro enthusiasts alike. The bar is open until late, ensuring a memorable night out in Pisa.

Mad Hatter Cocktail Bar

Tucked away on a quiet street near the Arno River, Mad Hatter Cocktail Bar is a hidden gem known for its inventive cocktails and whimsical ambiance. Inspired by Lewis Carroll's classic tale, Alice in Wonderland, the bar features eclectic decor, playful drink names, and a menu of expertly crafted cocktails. Guests can sip on concoctions such as the Cheshire Cat Cosmo or the Queen of Hearts Mojito while lounging in plush armchairs or mingling at the bar. With its quirky charm and imaginative cocktails, Mad Hatter Cocktail Bar offers a one-of-a-kind drinking experience in Pisa.

The Australian Pub

For a taste of Australia in the heart of Pisa, look no further than The Australian Pub. Located near the Leaning Tower, this lively establishment offers a laid-back atmosphere, friendly staff, and a selection of Australian beers and spirits. Guests can catch live sports on the big screen, play a game of billiards or darts, or simply relax with friends over a cold pint. The pub also serves up hearty Aussie-inspired dishes, including meat pies, sausage rolls, and Vegemite toast. Open until late, The Australian Pub is a popular hangout for both locals and travelers seeking a taste of Down Under in Pisa.

Caffè dell'Ussero
Dating back to the 18th century, Caffè dell'Ussero is one of Pisa's most iconic establishments, steeped in history and tradition. Located in Piazza Garibaldi, the historic cafe has welcomed patrons for centuries, including literary figures, artists, and intellectuals. Today, visitors can still enjoy the timeless elegance of Caffè dell'Ussero while savoring a coffee, aperitivo, or light meal. The cafe's outdoor terrace offers stunning views of the Arno River and the city's historic landmarks, making it a picturesque setting for a leisurely drink or a romantic evening. Caffè dell'Ussero is open throughout the day, welcoming guests to experience a taste of Pisa's rich cultural heritage.

From cozy hideaways to lively pubs, Pisa's bar scene offers a diverse array of experiences for visitors to enjoy. Whether you're in the mood for a classic pint at The Lions Fountain, a whimsical cocktail at Mad Hatter Cocktail Bar, or a taste of history at Caffè dell'Ussero, there's something for everyone

11.3 Nightclubs and Live Music Venues

As the sun sets over the picturesque city of Pisa, a vibrant nightlife scene comes alive, offering visitors an array of options for entertainment and enjoyment. From pulsating nightclubs to intimate live music venues, Pisa boasts a diverse selection of establishments where visitors can dance the night away or unwind to the sounds of talented musicians. Join me as we explore some of the top nightclubs and live music venues that Pisa has to offer.

1. Odeon Bistrot & Live Music

Located in the heart of Pisa's historic center, Odeon Bistrot & Live Music is a popular destination for those seeking live entertainment in an intimate setting. This cozy venue hosts a variety of musical performances, including jazz, blues, and acoustic sets, showcasing local talent as well as renowned artists. With its relaxed ambiance and eclectic lineup of acts, Odeon Bistrot & Live Music is the perfect spot to enjoy a night of great music and good company. The venue is open until late, providing a laid-back atmosphere for visitors to unwind and enjoy the sounds of Pisa's thriving music scene.

2. Borderline Club Pisa

For those looking to dance the night away, Borderline Club Pisa offers an electrifying nightlife experience in a dynamic setting. Located near the University of Pisa, this energetic nightclub features multiple dance floors, each playing a mix of house, techno, and hip-hop music to cater to different tastes. With its state-of-the-art sound system and immersive lighting effects, Borderline Club Pisa provides an unforgettable clubbing experience for partygoers. The club is open until the early hours of the morning, making it a popular destination for those seeking to dance until dawn.

3. The Jungle Pub

Situated in the lively San Martino district, The Jungle Pub is a laid-back establishment known for its relaxed atmosphere and eclectic mix of live music performances. From rock and reggae to indie and alternative, The Jungle Pub hosts a diverse lineup of bands and musicians, creating a vibrant hub for music lovers of all genres. With its cozy interior and outdoor terrace, the pub offers the perfect setting to enjoy a cold beer or cocktail while listening to live music. The Jungle Pub is open until late, making it a favorite haunt for both locals and visitors alike.

4. Exwide Club

Located on the outskirts of Pisa, Exwide Club is a sprawling entertainment complex that boasts multiple dance floors, bars, and outdoor areas for revelers to enjoy. The club offers a diverse range of music, with DJs playing everything from electronic and house to hip-hop and R&B, ensuring there's something for everyone to dance to. With its spacious layout and energetic atmosphere, Exwide Club offers an unforgettable clubbing experience for partygoers looking to let loose and have a great time. The club is open late into the night, providing ample opportunity for visitors to dance until the early hours.

5. Orzo Bruno

Tucked away in a historic building in Pisa's city center, Orzo Bruno is a charming cafe-bar that transforms into a lively music venue in the evenings. The venue hosts regular live music performances, ranging from acoustic sets and jazz nights to open mic sessions, showcasing local talent in an intimate setting. With its cozy interior and outdoor seating area, Orzo Bruno offers a relaxed atmosphere where visitors can enjoy great music, delicious drinks, and good company. The bar is open until late, making it a popular spot for an evening of entertainment in Pisa.

6. Barazzo Live Club

Situated in the vibrant San Francesco district, Barazzo Live Club is a dynamic venue that showcases a diverse range of live music acts and DJ sets throughout the week. From rock and punk to funk and soul, the club hosts an array of performances to cater to different musical tastes, ensuring there's always something exciting happening on stage. With its lively atmosphere and energetic crowds, Barazzo Live Club offers a thrilling nightlife experience for music enthusiasts and partygoers alike. The club is open until the early hours of the morning, providing plenty of opportunities to dance and enjoy the music until dawn.

From intimate live music venues to pulsating nightclubs, Pisa offers a vibrant nightlife scene that caters to diverse tastes and preferences. Whether you're looking to dance the night away at Borderline Club Pisa, unwind to the sounds of live music at Odeon Bistrot & Live Music, or enjoy a laid-back evening at The Jungle Pub, there's something for everyone to enjoy after dark in this captivating city. So, immerse yourself in the pulsating beats and electrifying atmosphere of Pisa's nightlife, and create unforgettable memories in the heart of Tuscany.

11.4 Cultural Performances and Shows

Pisa, with its rich history and vibrant cultural heritage, offers an array of cultural performances and shows that captivate visitors and locals alike. From classical concerts to contemporary theater productions, Pisa's cultural venues showcase a diverse range of artistic expressions. Let's delve into the city's cultural offerings and discover the venues where these performances unfold.

Teatro Verdi: A Hub of Theatrical Excellence

Located in the heart of Pisa, Teatro Verdi stands as a testament to the city's love for the performing arts. This historic theater, with its ornate architecture and plush interiors, hosts a variety of cultural performances, including opera, ballet, theater, and concerts. Renowned both nationally and internationally, Teatro Verdi is a must-visit destination for anyone seeking to immerse themselves in Pisa's vibrant cultural scene. With its diverse program and commitment to artistic excellence, Teatro Verdi promises an unforgettable cultural experience.

Palazzo Blu: Exhibitions and Art Installations

Palazzo Blu, situated along the Arno River, is not only a cultural center but also a venue for captivating exhibitions and art installations. This historic building regularly hosts temporary exhibitions featuring works by both local and international artists, spanning various genres and mediums. Visitors can explore the thought-provoking displays and engage with contemporary art in a dynamic and immersive environment. With its ever-changing lineup of exhibitions, Palazzo Blu offers a window into the dynamic world of contemporary art and culture.

Piazza dei Cavalieri: Historic Gatherings and Festivities

Steeped in history and tradition, Piazza dei Cavalieri serves as a focal point for cultural gatherings and festivities in Pisa. This picturesque square, surrounded by elegant palaces and historic buildings, provides a stunning backdrop for outdoor concerts, theatrical performances, and cultural events throughout the year. Visitors can soak in the vibrant atmosphere of the piazza while enjoying live music, dance performances, and other cultural spectacles. Whether attending a traditional festival or simply strolling through the square, Piazza dei Cavalieri offers a glimpse into Pisa's rich cultural heritage.

University of Pisa: Lectures and Academic Events
As one of the oldest universities in Italy, the University of Pisa is not only a center of academic excellence but also a hub of cultural activity. The university regularly hosts lectures, seminars, and academic conferences that cover a wide range of subjects, from literature and philosophy to science and technology. Visitors interested in intellectual pursuits and scholarly discussions can attend these events and engage with leading academics and experts in their fields. With its esteemed reputation and commitment to knowledge dissemination, the University of Pisa serves as a beacon of intellectual curiosity and cultural enrichment.

Churches and Cathedrals: Sacred Music Performances
Pisa's historic churches and cathedrals also play a significant role in the city's cultural landscape, often serving as venues for sacred music performances and choral concerts. Visitors can experience the transcendent beauty of Gregorian chants and classical compositions in the sublime acoustics of these sacred spaces. From the majestic Duomo di Pisa to the serene Church of Santa Maria della Spina, these architectural marvels provide a unique backdrop for spiritual and cultural experiences that resonate with visitors of all backgrounds.

In Pisa, cultural performances and shows offer a window into the city's rich history, artistic heritage, and contemporary creative expressions. Whether attending a theatrical production at Teatro Verdi, exploring cutting-edge art installations at Palazzo Blu, or experiencing the solemn beauty of sacred music in historic churches, visitors have ample opportunities to immerse themselves in Pisa's vibrant cultural scene. These cultural encounters not only entertain and inspire but also deepen our appreciation for the diverse traditions and artistic talents that define this enchanting city.

11.5 Safety Tips for Enjoying Pisa's Nightlife

As the sun sets over the picturesque city of Pisa, its vibrant nightlife scene comes to life, offering locals and visitors alike an array of entertainment options. From bustling bars and lively pubs to pulsating nightclubs, Pisa's nightlife has something for everyone. However, as with any city, it's essential to prioritize safety while enjoying the vibrant atmosphere of Pisa after dark. Here are some invaluable safety tips to ensure a memorable and safe nightlife experience in Pisa.

Stay Aware of Your Surroundings

Before delving into the excitement of Pisa's nightlife, it's crucial to stay aware of your surroundings at all times. While Pisa is generally a safe city, it's wise to remain vigilant, especially in crowded areas and late at night. Keep an eye on your belongings, such as bags and wallets, and avoid displaying valuable items openly.

Travel in Groups

One of the best ways to enhance safety while enjoying Pisa's nightlife is to travel in groups. Whether you're exploring the city's bars, pubs, or nightclubs, having companions by your side adds an extra layer of security. Stick together with your friends and watch out for each other throughout the evening.

Plan Your Transportation in Advance

Before heading out for a night on the town, it's essential to plan your transportation in advance. Consider how you'll get to and from your destinations safely, especially if you'll be indulging in alcohol. Pisa offers various transportation options, including taxis, rideshare services, and public transportation. Alternatively, if you're staying within walking distance, opt for a leisurely stroll to soak in the city's nighttime ambiance.

Moderate Alcohol Consumption

While enjoying Pisa's nightlife, it's easy to get caught up in the festivities and indulge in alcoholic beverages. However, it's essential to consume alcohol responsibly and in moderation. Pace yourself throughout the evening, alternate alcoholic drinks with water, and know your limits to avoid overindulgence. Additionally, be mindful of the local drinking laws and regulations in Pisa.

Choose Well-Lit and Populated Areas

When exploring Pisa's nightlife, prioritize venues and areas that are well-lit and populated. Opt for established bars, pubs, and nightclubs that have a positive reputation and attract a diverse crowd. Avoid dark alleys and secluded areas, especially if you're unfamiliar with the surroundings.

Trust Your Instincts

Above all, trust your instincts while enjoying Pisa's nightlife. If something feels off or uncomfortable, don't hesitate to remove yourself from the situation and seek assistance if necessary. Whether it's a crowded dance floor or a late-night stroll through the city streets, prioritize your safety and well-being at all times.

As you immerse yourself in the vibrant nightlife of Pisa, remember to prioritize safety and responsible behavior. By staying aware of your surroundings, traveling in groups, planning transportation in advance, moderating alcohol consumption, choosing well-lit areas, and trusting your instincts, you can ensure a memorable and safe experience while enjoying all that Pisa's nightlife has to offer. So, embrace the excitement of the city after dark while keeping safety at the forefront of your adventures.

CONCLUSION AND INSIDER TIPS FOR VISITORS

Congratulations! You've reached the end of **"Pisa Travel Guide 2024 And Beyond,"** a comprehensive resource crafted with love and passion for exploration. As a seasoned traveler and author, I've poured my heart into uncovering the gems of Pisa, ensuring that your journey through this enchanting city is nothing short of extraordinary. Now, as you prepare to embark on your own adventure, let me leave you with some insider tips to enhance your experience and make the most of your time in Pisa.

Embrace the Unexpected

Pisa is a city brimming with surprises around every corner. While the Leaning Tower may be the iconic symbol that draws visitors from far and wide, don't be afraid to wander off the beaten path and discover the lesser-known wonders of Pisa. From hidden courtyards to quaint cafés tucked away in narrow alleyways, embracing the unexpected is the key to unlocking the true essence of this captivating city.

Timing is Everything

To truly savor the magic of Pisa, timing is everything. While the city is beautiful year-round, consider visiting during the shoulder seasons of spring and autumn when the weather is mild, the crowds are thinner, and the city comes alive with vibrant festivals and cultural events. Additionally, plan your visit to iconic landmarks like the Leaning Tower during off-peak hours to avoid long queues and enjoy a more intimate experience.

Engage with the Locals

One of the greatest joys of travel is connecting with the locals and immersing yourself in the culture of your destination. In Pisa, don't hesitate to strike up conversations with friendly locals, whether it's at a bustling market or a family-owned trattoria. Their insights and recommendations can lead you to hidden gems and authentic experiences that you won't find in any guidebook.

Indulge in Culinary Delights

No trip to Pisa is complete without indulging in its culinary delights. From freshly baked focaccia to creamy gelato, Pisa's food scene is a feast for the senses. Venture beyond the tourist traps and seek out trattorias and osterias favored by locals, where you can savor traditional Tuscan dishes made with love and passed down through generations.

Pack Light and Comfortably

As you prepare for your journey to Pisa, remember to pack light and comfortably. The city's cobblestone streets and narrow alleys can be challenging to navigate with bulky luggage, so opt for a compact suitcase or backpack that allows for easy mobility. And don't forget to pack comfortable walking shoes – exploring Pisa on foot is the best way to soak in its beauty and charm.

Respect the Heritage

Finally, as you explore the historic landmarks and cultural treasures of Pisa, remember to respect the city's rich heritage and traditions. Whether you're admiring the Leaning Tower or strolling through the Piazza dei Miracoli, take a moment to pause, reflect, and appreciate the centuries of history and craftsmanship that have shaped this remarkable city.

As you turn the final pages of "Pisa Travel Guide 2024 and Beyond," I hope you feel inspired and excited to embark on your own adventure in this timeless city. With its iconic landmarks, vibrant culture, and warm hospitality, Pisa offers a wealth of experiences waiting to be discovered. So pack your bags, follow your curiosity, and prepare to create memories that will last a lifetime. Safe travels, and may your journey through Pisa be filled with wonder, joy, and unforgettable moments.

PISA TRAVEL PLANNER

NAME:
_____

DEPARTURE DATE:
_____

RETURN DATE:
_____

MY PACKING LIST

- _____
- _____
- _____
- _____
- _____
- _____
- _____
- _____
- _____
- _____

MY TRAVEL BUDGET

A-7 DAY TRAVEL ITINERARIES PLANNING

DAY 1:

_____

_____

_____

_____

_____

DAY 2:

_____

_____

_____

_____

_____

DAY 3:

_____

_____

_____

_____

_____

DAY 4:

DAY 5:

DAY 6:

DAY 7

MUST-DO THINGS IN PISA

-
-
-
-
-
-
-
-
-
-
-
-
-
-
-
-
-

MUST-TRY FOOD IN PISA

-
-
-
-
-
-
-
-
-
-
-
-
-
-
-
-
-

LIST OF TOURIST SITES & HIDDEN GEMS TO VISIT IN PISA

SHARE YOUR PISA TRAVEL EXPERIENCE

Printed in Great Britain
by Amazon